"The average tenure for a CISO today is two and a half years. Any CISO who reads this book and uses it as a guide will extend that average. Through his entertaining narration of experiences and their outcomes, Barak Engel brings the reader to the inevitable conclusion that integrating security into business practices should never be an adversarial process with internal partners.

With this book, Barak shatters the myth that successful CISOs have to be technologists first and foremost—without attention to the role that security can play in facilitating business goals and objectives. His well-written and humorous anecdotes and musings make it crystal clear that a good CISO is a business enabler, and he provides experiential guidance on what that means in today's threat environment."

Greg Reber, *CEO, AsTech*

"In the realm of cybersecurity, Barak champions the human perspective, a viewpoint often overlooked. The key lies in recognition; Overloading individuals with jargon and a multitude of problems simultaneously reduces the motivation. People thrive on logic; they need to understand the underlying problem and its significance in the cybersecurity landscape to feel motivated to solve it. Throughout history, the most groundbreaking inventions emerged from human motivation, evident in creations like Linux, Git, Falco, Wahuz, and Kubernetes, etc. Barak advocates prioritizing cybersecurity issues logically and introduces gamification—an approach that taps into our inherent love for healthy competition and recognition. His innovative proposal of a leaderboard provides the acknowledgment individuals crave. Research attests that completing tasks brings immense satisfaction, and people have a finite capacity to solve problems daily. Barak, by uniting these ideas, has provided a fresh perspective that could revolutionize cybersecurity practices."

Anshu Bansal, *CEO, CloudDefense.AI*

"What sets this book apart is its authenticity. It clearly defines how a CISO helps drive the business to innovate and grow. It prompts a mindset shift that every executive should come to understand about the true value of good cybersecurity in modern business."

Mike Hamilton, *VP of IT, Cruise*

"*Why CISOs Fail* by Barak Engel is an absolute gem in the world of cybersecurity literature. Engel's writing style is captivating, drawing readers in with a delightful blend of humor and playfulness. It's a rare treat to find a book on such a serious subject that manages to infuse fun into its pages while maintaining the utmost professionalism. Engel's prose is as engaging as it is informative, making this book a joy to read. What truly sets *Why CISOs Fail* apart is its ability to inject the much-needed human element into the realm of information security. I've personally found the insight offered in the book to be a contributing factor in elevating my own mindset in approaching information security with a central focus on people and the business. The results have been nothing short of remarkable with stakeholders delighted with the realized outcomes.

Engel takes a thoughtful approach to dissecting the challenges Chief Information Security Officers face, offering profound insights into the personal and organizational dynamics that often go unnoticed. This book not only educates but also empathizes with the individuals tasked with safeguarding our digital world. It's a must-read for anyone in the field, and even those outside of it will find themselves thoroughly engrossed and enlightened by Engel's unique perspective. In a world where the stakes are high and the margin for error slim, *Why CISOs Fail* is a breath of fresh air that should be celebrated and widely shared. In this updated edition, Barak expands further on the first edition and introduces two pivotal concepts for security management that are poised to further solidify *Why CISOs Fail* as an essential reference for anyone seeking to navigate the complex landscape of information security with intelligence and finesse. I highly recommend this book to anyone curious about the information security field and strongly encourage it for members of my team and cross-functional security partners."

Michael Choui, *CEO, Atlas One*

"Barak's book offers refreshing perspectives on how to focus an information security program on business risk. His experiences shine through. If you are looking for academic concepts, look elsewhere. Barak offers real-world, pragmatic advice. This book is a great resource for CISOs, IT leaders and Information Security practitioners!"

Gideon T. Rasmussen, *CISSP, CRISC, CISA, CISM, CIPP*

"Barak's real-world stories paint a true picture into the role of the CISO as a business enabler. Reading, digesting, and learning from those scenarios alone will add years of experience to any aspiring CISO's skills. A fantastic piece!"

Branden R. Williams, *DBA, CISSP, CISM,*
Author and Cybersecurity Expert

"Life sometimes offers us mentors and friends, people who will suggest that you may be doing the wrong things or that you don't even have the right objectives. Barak's book highlights how technical security management is a case of asymmetric warfare and that no system is good enough to withstand all attacks all the time. His words explore where CISOs find themselves today and in the future, managing customers, the board, and legal expectations. He articulates the problem of third-party cloud dependency and provides useful clear advice such as 'what to ask your cloud vendor.' We learn about the 'power of negative inference thinking,' and the art of selling to the business versus selling to a customer. Barak leaves the reader empowered to partner with sales, leveraging security as a critical feature set driving upsell opportunities. My favorite takeaway from this reading was understanding what people say versus what they want. Spend a day with a security guru and enjoy the journey into the mind of a modern-day CISO."

Robin Basham, *M.IT, M.Ed., CISSP, CISA, CGEIT,*
CRISC, CEO/CISO EnterpriseGRC Solutions

"Forget CISOs. This book is a must-read for every CEO who's serious about security and who needs to understand the challenges faced by their own Chief Protection Officer."

Neal O'Farrell, *Founder, Brainisphere,*
Executive director of the identity-theft council

"You know, Barak, people sometimes ask me to read what they had written, and it's kinda awkward, because that stuff isn't usually very good, and how do you tell them that? But I found myself engaged all the way through, really enjoying the writing, the tales and the humor, and even feeling like I understand what's going on. That's so neat!"

Some guy called Ed

Why CISOs Fail

Released in 2017, the first edition of *Why CISOs Fail* reimagined the role of the Chief Information Security Officer in a new and powerful way. Written to be easily consumable by both security pros as well as everyone who must deal with them, the book explores the different realms in which security leaders fail to deliver meaningful impact to their organizations, and why this happens. Its central thesis—that security is primarily a human behavioral discipline rather than a technology one—has been gaining increased attention as a core tenet of the field, and the book was ultimately inducted into the cybersecurity canon as a leading book on security management.

In this freshly updated edition, Barak Engel adds new sections that correspond with the chapters of the original book: security as a discipline; as a business enabler; in sales; in legal; in compliance; in technology; and as an executive function. He explores new ideas in each operational area, providing essential insights into emerging aspects of the discipline. He then proposes two critical concepts for security management—the concept of "digital shrinkage" and the transition from CISO to CI/SO—that together offer a new paradigm for any organization that wants to become truly successful in its security journey.

Why CISOs (Still) *Fail* is delivered in Barak's conversational, humoristic style that has attracted a global audience to this and his other book, *The Security Hippie*. As he notes, the book's goal is to entertain as much as to inform, and he dearly hopes that you have fun reading it.

Barak Engel brings over three decades of information security experience into his writings. As the originator of the vCISO concept, he has served in the CISO role in dozens of organizations such as Stubhub, Mulesoft, Amplitude Analytics, and BetterUp, and his consulting firm, EAmmune, has managed security for hundreds of brands globally. A sought-after speaker and writer, he has made numerous contributions to the field with his thought-provoking insights about security as a business enabler, leading to the induction in 2021 of *Why CISOs Fail* into the Cybercannon. Barak serves on multiple security company advisory boards and is a member of the Theia Institute, a security think tank.

Security, Audit and Leadership Series

Series Editor: Dan Swanson, Dan Swanson and Associates, Ltd., Winnipeg, Manitoba, Canada.

The **Security, Audit and Leadership Series** publishes leading-edge books on critical subjects facing security and audit executives as well as business leaders. Key topics addressed include Leadership, Cybersecurity, Security Leadership, Privacy, Strategic Risk Management, Auditing IT, Audit Management and Leadership

Auditing Information and Cyber Security Governance: A Controls-Based Approach
Robert E. Davis

The Security Leader's Communication Playbook: Bridging the Gap between Security and the Business
Jeffrey W. Brown

Modern Management and Leadership: Best Practice Essentials with CISO/CSO Applications
Mark Tarallo

Rising from the Mailroom to the Boardroom: Unique Insights for Governance, Risk, Compliance and Audit Leaders
Bruce Turner

Operational Auditing: Principles and Techniques for a Changing World (Second Edition)
Hernan Murdock

CyRM℠: Mastering the Management of Cybersecurity
David X Martin

Why CISOs Fail (Second Edition)
Barak Engel

Why CISOs Fail

Second Edition

Barak Engel

CRC Press
Taylor & Francis Group
Boca Raton London New York

CRC Press is an imprint of the
Taylor & Francis Group, an **informa** business

Designed cover image: © Shutterstock

Second edition published 2024
by CRC Press
2385 NW Executive Center Drive, Suite 320, Boca Raton FL 33431

and by CRC Press
4 Park Square, Milton Park, Abingdon, Oxon, OX14 4RN

CRC Press is an imprint of Taylor & Francis Group, LLC

© 2024 Barak Engel

First edition published by CRC Press 2018

Library of Congress Cataloging-in-Publication Data
Names: Engel, Barak, author.
Title: Why CISOs fail / Barak Engel.
Description: Second Edition. | Boca Raton : CRC Press, 2024. |
Series: Security, audit and leadership series |
Revised edition of the author's Why CISOs fail, 2018.
Identifiers: LCCN 2023042155 (print) | LCCN 2023042156 (ebook) |
ISBN 9781032299259 (hardback) | ISBN 9781032299273 (paperback) |
ISBN 9781003302759 (ebook)
Subjects: LCSH: Chief information officers. | Information technology–Management. |
Computer networks–Security measures. | Computer security. | Data protection.
Classification: LCC HD30.2 .E5394 2024 (print) |
LCC HD30.2 (ebook) | DDC 658.4/78–dc23/eng/20230908
LC record available at https://lccn.loc.gov/2023042155
LC ebook record available at https://lccn.loc.gov/2023042156

ISBN: 9781032299259 (hbk)
ISBN: 9781032299273 (pbk)
ISBN: 9781003302759 (ebk)

DOI: 10.1201/9781003302759

Typeset in Caslon
by Newgen Publishing UK

Contents

Foreword

When you read this, I will have been a CISO for over a year. In no small part, that tenure—and my ongoing development—is thanks to Barak Engel and *Why CISOs Fail*. It's almost cliché—as this year progressed, the lessons seemed to return at just the right time. My nearly chronic imposter syndrome faded, anxiety morphed into intense curiosity, and my confidence continued to grow. My job has been remarkably fulfilling and, thankfully, the kind of exciting most CISOs prefer.

My association's growth often matches that of the cybersecurity industry, on a cycle of perpetual escalation. Our board created a stand-alone CISO role and function, shifting me away from my decade-long CIO and operations duties. I wanted to level up to match their expectations—plus, hundreds of thousands of CompTIA-certified cyber pros would expect nothing less. I ordered a tall stack of books, some of which are the inches-thick volumes we all love to hate. When the books arrived, *Why CISOs Fail* had the best and most provocative title and required far fewer trees to print. Plus, starting with a concise and witty author had to make for a great start.

As you start the book, you immediately realize Barak is genuine, gracious, and gregarious—and he happens to work at the highest levels in cybersecurity. I've spoken with him several times, immediately hitting it off on personal and professional matters. He's disarming, quite the opposite of a typically rigid guardian of the keys to a digital kingdom. To him, information security is accessible, valuable, and slightly misunderstood. *Why CISO's Fail* and the follow-up *The Security Hippie* foster camaraderie with the reader and the characters in each story. Barak wants you to be successful and fulfill what can be a fantastic role. His books irrevocably changed how I view CISOs and information security overall. His viewpoint will change you too.

It's not a surprise that Barak believes InfoSec, at its core, is risk management rather than simply information assurance. Where things get interesting, though, is his take on technological risk beyond the rigid constraints of traditional information security practices. Barak's practical approach offers a simple framework—people, technology, operations, and privacy/compliance. His rubric makes for effortless conversations. It's a subtle and sublime shift: "I work to decrease undue tech risk to help businesses win" vs. "I work in Information Security to secure our data." With the first, I've had unexpectedly deep conversations that led to novel and lasting impacts across the business. I still talk about InfoSec too—it's my go-to for a quick exit at cocktail parties.

While Barak's perspective makes the industry and role approachable, CISOs do have a hard job with a steep and unyielding learning curve. When the job feels overwhelming for me, Barak's principles steady the ship, the first being that there is nothing inherently special about cybersecurity. If you knock out the notion that you have a magic, elevated status, others perceive that you are looking for a shared outcome. Rather than being the strong arm of the law, you are a de facto Chief Risk Officer for your company. You enable others and are not an end to yourself. As you read, I'd encourage you to think hard about his philosophy. As you work, I'd urge you to do more than just think hard about it.

What emerges when you buy in is an earned and permanent seat at the table rather than feeling like you're avoided or endured. Others treat you and your function with the respect and due care it demands because they know how important it has been and will be to them. The cycle gets even stronger as you get more calls about brand-new business matters fueled by your positive and enduring perspective. And yes, each of those happened to me and my function in Year One.

Here's the personal gift that Barak's book gave me. I needed the CISO move more than I knew—for my literal sanity. I've battled mental illness most of my life. While I have the acumen and experience for building technology and operations, types of operational stress can hit me hard. Too much stress isn't healthy for anyone. With no end to InfoSec threats and the stakes rising daily, accepting a job designed perhaps to be a convenient scapegoat or one with a chance of catastrophe could be particularly bizarre.

Why CISOs Fail is a key to mental strength for me, with strategic insight into traditional pain points and how to avoid them. I might have previously sent myself into a tailspin worrying about a catastrophic miss far outside my control. Instead, summarized throughout the book, we prepare, listen, advise and respond. We work on how to get to the right place, never leading with "No." We diligently and empathetically tailor and implement the processes and procedures built by giants before us, acting as partners rather than police. We involve the entire business in managing and responding to technology risk. We acknowledge that complete perfection is impossible and instead train for what truly matters. Worry then morphs into a broad and proactive outlook, and stress instead has a productive and pragmatic channel.

I grew up during the era of the ridiculous 'No Fear' t-shirts and bumper stickers. In stark contrast to those macho slogans, Infosec needs a healthy fear. With the next vulnerability lurking around the corner, Barak's toolset and notions of resilience bring added and reliable firepower that keeps fear at bay. We are on the hook for taking stock of our businesses, advising on that risk in ways anyone can understand. We seek to build strong and sustainable solutions and ultimately serve as trusted advisors and strong practitioners. We view risk without hysterics, collaborate rather than indict and use the position as a license for how to grow rather than screaming "No."

I've read each of Barak's books once through—there is no time to repeat them yet as there is much to learn inside the inches-thick tomes I ordered. However, absorbing and applying all of the above has persisted and continues. Barak's approach makes intuitive sense and it works in a practical, daily setting.

The power of this book is that the chapters weave together like a fabric I can wear every day, and it still fits very well. After reading this book and the follow-up *The Security Hippie*, I reached out to Barak to thank him for illuminating a path I didn't expect to find. From personal experience, after you read the book, pay attention to Barak's voice as you do the job. I suspect you'll be writing him a thank-you note too.

—**Randy Gross,** *CISO and CIO at CompTIA*

Preface

Let me tell you a story.

We were about to start our weekly security program meeting when Dario brought it up. "Congratulations, man!"

Even through the Zoom window, he seemed genuinely excited.

"For what?" I wondered.

Nothing happened in my life that would merit a congratulatory note. Not that Dario would know. It was deep into the still scary, highly isolating stage of the COVID-19 pandemic, a few weeks following one of the most depressing Christmas holiday periods I can recall. The pandemic economy was minting winners and losers all over the place, and the particular company involved was unfortunately on the latter side. Dario was one of a couple of holdouts after they recently let go of most of their staff.

That I was still there was a positive surprise to me personally, but surely he couldn't be that cynical.

"Your book!" He gushed.

My book? I was still a year away from the publication of *The Security Hippie* and had only started writing it – partly because the very same Dario inspired me to do so (a story I share in that book).

"What book? What are you talking about?"

His face took on a look of astonishment. "You don't know?"

I shook my head.

"Your book. *Why CISOs Fail.* It's in the Cybercannon."

"Wait, what?!"

As a repeat offender, I can confidently say that writing trade books like this one must be a labor of love, or at least it's not done for money, because there isn't any in it. Motivations will vary; for me, *Why CISOs Fail* was an attempt to share key insights I'd gained over decades of serving in the capacity of fractional CISO (a.k.a vCISO) in many organizations.

I kept it short and accessible, asked and answered one question—the one in the title. That it needed an entire book to do so is a clear indicator of how important it is to me. But it's hard for these kinds of books to gain recognition, and I'm not good at self-promoting. Still, somehow, it found an audience, and that audience kept growing.

One of my best moments came when my friend Lance sent me a photo from the NY subway of somebody sitting across from him, reading *Why CISOs Fail.* In his text, he said the fella was laughing every couple of minutes, which was precisely what I was hoping to achieve with the book's overall tone. It felt amazing.

Then, at some point, someone I hadn't known who had that power saw fit to nominate it into the cannon. I had no idea it was happening, and it led directly to this second edition.

So let me tell you what it's actually about, beyond a way to put that nice logo on the cover.

It's a response to the feedback I'd received over the years from many parties. People who have done more than I could ever do to promote *Why CISOs Fail* by telling others about it. Readers who reached out to me over LinkedIn because they felt so inspired. This includes Randy Gross, whom I only met because he read and loved the original book. So much so, that I felt compelled to invite him to write the new foreword.

By and large, they liked that it was short—but they wanted more anyway. Especially more stories.

Good luck sorting that schizo message out.

As I revisited the original text, I realized that most of it is still just as relevant today as it was back when I first wrote it. It didn't grow stale;

if anything, it became more relevant. And that provided me with the key inspiration for how to construct a second edition unlike any other second edition I'd ever read—and allowed me to square that circle. It would be a bit longer, but you could easily distinguish between old and new.

What if, on top of making the necessary updates, I added shorter, half chapters to each of the original ones, with all new content? Since the chapters each already covered individual topics, it would be easy to maintain the theme. I proposed it to the good people at Taylor & Francis, and in their virtual slanty-eyed shoulder-shrugging sort of way they said "sure, go for it."

They already knew I can't do anything the normal way.

Then the idea of identifying the half chapters with the ".2" at the end came into life, a nod and a wink towards all the software engineers out there, and a way to easily support further editions; surely you can see the arrival of the ".3"s. Since I am nothing if not responsive to my audience, there are plenty of new stories; if you like those, really check out *The Security Hippie*. Also, in keeping the tradition from the first edition, one of the chapters is written by a new external contributor, the wonderful (and frighteningly smart) Dr. Todd Jacobs.

Most importantly, the last chapter offers a new paradigm for thinking about security management. And in that, I feel that this second edition provides a better, more comprehensive answer to the question of "why CISOs fail" than I ever could imagine when I wrote the original.

It is my sincerest hope, whether you are new to *Why CISOs Fail*, or bought this new edition because you loved the first and wondered what new and outrageous thing I might say here, that you will enjoy these pages. And please, don't hesitate to let me know!

Thank you for coming along this journey.

With my love and appreciation to all of you,

—Barak

O
Why?

Is security and privacy something that's on your mind?

It must be, or you wouldn't have opened this book.

Why are you thinking about it? What does information security mean to you?

We are at an age where business, in practically every sector, is transforming rapidly due to the technology revolution; where governments must contend with threats that didn't really exist before; where "warfare" is increasingly spoken about in conjunction with the prefix "cyber;" and where bullying of all forms (including "cancelling") is faster and more devastating due to social media.

It didn't use to be like this. Just a few short years ago, you could keep things you wanted to keep to yourself private. Information, that most powerful weapon of all, could be kept hidden in a safe, away from most curious minds, except maybe those of professional spies, who played a complex game most of us would only read about in John Le Carré novels.

Now you can't even get a fake news story, let alone legitimate leaks of valid information, removed from circulation, even if they are highly damaging to you. And let's not even start with deepfakes, manufactured videos in the likeness of real people.

So how do you do business in this brave new world?

And just as importantly, who do you trust to keep you safe?

Surely, you could choose to ignore this issue. And it might even work out fine for a while until some mysterious figure halfway across the world shuts down your technology operations, which is when you discover that you really can't do business anymore without all that computer stuff. Then they demand millions in ransom, and no matter how many times you call your IT guy, they can't help you.

DOI: 10.1201/9781003302759-1

1

Or maybe you've thought ahead, and instead of the IT guy, you call the security expert. The person appointed to prevent this very thing from happening. The one who has been telling you for years that this might happen, and whose budget seems to increase faster than even your healthcare premiums do.

And they *still* can't help you.

In frustration, you agree with the rapid-fire decision that they should be fired. The resulting feeling of satisfaction lasts for a few minutes, until reality rudely intrudes again.

What next?

Maybe you haven't suffered a breach yet. You're doing the right thing and sitting in a meeting of the executive committee, or perhaps with the board, trying to have an informed conversation on this topic. You bring in experts to tell you what to do. But it doesn't make any sense. All they seem to want to talk about is technology and associated expenditures. Isn't that what the CIO should be handling? You look at the CIO sideways. They are staring at their phone and seem to be ignoring you.

Or maybe you've all had these experiences and conversations and decided to hire a new executive—the *Chief Information Security Officer* (CISO). Heck, maybe you already hired them. Yet all they seem to do is—you guessed it—talk about software and compliance and class-action lawsuits and frightening headlines of breaches. They are always in a sour mood and are not team players (to put it mildly). You feel constantly bullied into signing off on significant technology expenditures, but the conversation never changes, they never seem satisfied, and nothing ever improves.

You certainly don't feel any safer.

How is that possible?

Do these people even know what they are doing?

Or maybe, just maybe, you are the CISO. You feel like nobody ever listens to you or takes you seriously. You show them, and they ignore you. All the facts are on your side. You see things. You know things. Scary things. Real threats to the business. Why won't they listen unless you threaten them with compliance mandates? And in the back of your mind, you also know the truth: no matter how well you do, you're the one who will get fired when something goes wrong. It's an unspoken part of your employment contract. You might even get prosecuted and convicted, as happened to Joe Sullivan, the CISO at Uber.

So tell me . . . how's that bourbon?

This book tries to address these topics. We will take a tour via the various aspects of managing the discipline of information security and highlight how we've been going at it in all the wrong ways. We, the practitioners in the field, have been putting the technology aspects of the discipline ahead of the needs of the business, failing and even dogmatically refusing to acknowledge the reality of business operations. We, the hiring committees, keep looking for the wrong candidates, and finding plenty of them to fill the role. We, the executives, fail to take advantage of the uniquely helpful capabilities that security people bring to the table when it comes to critical decision making.

We can all do better.

But first, let me share a personal story, about how my formal career in security started.

"You've done security before, right?"

I was sitting in my typical Silicon Valley office. An actual office, mind you—while open-space was becoming all the rage, it still had not infected every company to the degree that it has today, and line management types like me tended to have an enclosed space to call home. Mine was an 8 by 12 room that somehow managed to fit three desks for the three managers who shared it. There was the network manager, the systems manager, and me, the operations manager, the one who was responsible for making sure the other guys' stuff was actually doing what it was supposed to do, day in and day out.

Later on I managed to score my own office, nicknamed "the closet" because it was a tiny room, and we could not resist the temptation to name it after its original purpose as a janitorial closet. When I first floated the idea, I simply asked if I could move into the "hallway closet." The nickname stuck. But it was just big enough to fit a working environment and had one big advantage in not being shared. Naive as I was, I actually thought that the practice of information security called for some privacy, and I thought it passionately enough that I managed to convince the CIO of it as well.

It was Friday evening, and I was wrapping up a couple of emails before heading home. The office was mostly empty. The operations team were in their "pit," which was another shared office, but other than that, there were maybe one or two others in the building. One of them turned out to be the CIO, and she was the one standing at my door, asking me if I knew something about security.

"*Well, yeah ... you know that*", I answered. "*Not formally, of course, but ...*"

"*I need your help,*" she cut me off, rather abruptly. She generally had an abrupt manner, but I immediately sensed that this was different.

What I didn't know at that moment was that, in handling the breach that brought down half of the company's platform that weekend, I would effectively be relaunching my career. Like many old-timer security folks, my technical background was in coding and networking—an exploding growth discipline in the late '80s and throughout the '90s, and one that was a natural extension of my youth spent tinkering with technology in unintended ways. I grew up when "hacker" was considered mostly as an alternate term for "nerd who understands computers and command lines," and when being one was considered cool and popularized by movies like *War Games* (still one of my all-time favorites). I programmed (in machine language, no less) and war-dialed, sure, but a good friend and I had also rigged together a dual expansion card for the Apple II platform that allowed us to tap into and parse communications from early information networks that connected major banks and other institutions, just to see what was going on. Those were the days when "hackers"—using the word in its very naive mid-'80s sense—like me actually added our real home phone number to the little "cracked by" screen that we would add to a computer game we made available for copying, just so other folks like us could call and introduce themselves. My "cracker handle" was a literal translation in Hebrew of the phrase "pain in the ass." There were no laws against doing that at the time, and curiosity did not kill the proverbial kitties. If anything, it just made us more curious.

When the Internet took center stage, I was more than ready. It was no shock that I ended up working for an ISP straight out of university in late 1994, although it was entirely by mistake. I arrived for an interview at a company that was building computer parts, and simply entered the wrong door. The person I ran into, who later became my boss and first important career mentor, asked me if I knew anything about networking. My answer had him sit me down in a room for a 2-hour interview, which resulted in a job offer on the spot. Amusingly enough, I never even realized it was the wrong company until after the interview was over!

That was the start of my formal networking career.

We managed to resolve the breach that weekend. The security officer—the fact that the company actually had one was a testament to advanced thinking—could not be reached at all, but we put together a team, ran the forensic analysis, cleaned everything up, and recovered the platform by the wee hours of Monday morning, with no interruption to customers. I finally went home around 4 a.m. that day.

By the following Friday, I was promoted to head of Information Security, a new department that I was supposed to build from scratch. That weekend and the next 12 months were incredibly educational and laid the foundation for my next career, that of trusted security advisor and consultant to corporations large and small. It was often in the role of "virtual CISO" (vCISO), with the goal of helping companies understand the proper role of a CISO in their organization and how to structure a program around this unintuitive discipline that often seems at odds with every other in the business. Other elements of the role included helping and mentoring others inside those organizations who were working to develop a career in information security, many of whom I am immensely proud to have known, worked and shared ideas with, and whose careers have already taken them to incredible heights.

This is a book about ideas, borne of countless experiences and observations, conversations, and debates. I don't pretend to know everything about security, and I am still learning every single day, with every interaction with our clients and their boards, my peers and colleagues (and critics), and my mentors and mentees. I do know, however, that these ideas can be helpful, because I have observed and experienced their empirical success. I have been told countless times by the poor folks who have heard me pontificate over the years about security management that "they wished there was a book about it" so they could read it to help prepare them for their chosen careers. I have been told by senior executives and board members, in both technology and non-technology disciplines, that their boards need to hear what I had to say, so they could make better decisions, pleading with me to "share something with them that they could forward." I've heard from participants in my presentations that the questions I asked made them wonder about and reevaluate their jobs, and later on, from the subset of those people who actually bothered to look me up and let me know how much happier they became as a result. This book is my attempt to respond collectively to everyone.

I mention boards, for boards today are placed in a tricky position, where what feels like a highly technical field that should have no play in the boardroom seems to take an ever increasingly large portion of meetings. Indeed, boards are in danger of doing too much and too little at the same time, something we will cover at some length, and which can be dangerous to any firm. I've spoken in board meetings, often in single-slide, 5-minute segments, to try and help close the vast chasm between the strategic understanding of the company's business and the often tactical nature of security. This is a discipline that can have a major impact on the business but is shrouded in mystery as to how, exactly, the tactics apply to the strategy—let alone that it should be the other way around. With new SEC rules demanding cyber experience on boards, it's only getting more challenging.

This book is for all of you, and for anyone else interested in security. It is not intended to be technical, nor academic. It is, though, most certainly intended to be entertaining.

Before we proceed, however, it is worth stating that I stand, without question, on the shoulders of giants. Yet maybe the concepts we will discuss combined with a less intimidating delivery focused on the business and not on the practice of security as a technology discipline will make this topic a little less sensational and a little more accessible.

If so, I will have succeeded.

Last, I am including many personal "war stories" in this book, based on my experiences from the field. They are all real, but details are often (1) changed at least enough to obscure the sources and protect the innocent; and (2) dramatized a bit to make them easier to digest and more entertaining to read. After all, security doesn't have to be boring!

1
THE DISMAL DISCIPLINE

"We're looking for a CISO."

This phrase has become increasingly common these days. I hear it so often that seemingly not a day goes by without someone saying that to me, be it a recruiter, potential client, or frustrated colleague through LinkedIn.

I can't say that this is a bad thing. Clearly, finding yourself in what appears to be a maelstrom of demand is always a healthy thing for one's career prospects.

And yet, it is almost inevitable that, when I ask a few basic questions about the goals for the role, it transpires that they view it as some sort of "really smart guy" (women do go into security, but unfortunately, it appears like it is even rarer in Information Security than in other technology disciplines) who "can figure out what we need to do to protect our systems."

Which, to clarify, means doing so with technology, often—formally or otherwise—as part of the IT department. Sadly, in the years since this book first came out, this trend has simply become more pronounced.

One particular conversation I had took place in the offices of a very large technology firm and household name. The CIO, a sharp and lively fellow, asked me how I viewed the role of a CISO. I explained that I thought of it as a business partner to all departments. As someone who can help the organization understand and manage underlying risks in business operations, hidden liabilities, brand management, and service agreements. Someone who could also help uncover ways to promote the brand further by enhancing consumer trust, engaging externally with the customer base and the media on emerging issues like personal information privacy and data portability.

He looked at me and said, "I like it, but don't you think that the main role is to protect the company?"

I knew what he meant. He tried to get me to talk about technology. Firewalls, benchmarks, intrusion detection, immutable virtual containers.

"Of course," I answered, and then added, "But I think that protecting the company means all of these things and more." Guessing where his mind was going, I added, "You see, as a CISO, I never focus on technology, because technology is implemented to serve a business purpose, not as a business goal unto itself. Even if your business is technology, your ultimate goal is still to sell as much of it as possible, isn't it?"

He became increasingly uncomfortable.

They ended up promoting a technologist internally into the role of CISO, and from all I can tell, three technologists in the role later, nothing has really changed, even though they were gasping for change.

The fact that security budgets are taking an ever-larger portion of IT budgets (again, formally or otherwise) only serves to reinforce the notion that security is a technology problem. The challenge here is twofold: first, the mistaken notion that security problems are generally solved via technology; and second, the even more mistaken notion that security is a technology problem in the first place.

It shouldn't be.

A big reason why is simply that, when viewed in this fashion, security also tends to primarily serve as a business stopper. Security technology solutions are, by and large, focused on the prevention of something bad from happening. Distressingly, it increasingly seems like technology pros have come to understand security primarily in the context of *confidentiality*, which, even if all you do is follow the oldest established approaches to security, neglects *integrity* and *availability* (also known as the CIA model).

In reality, bad things don't happen in a vacuum. Rather, bad things are allowed to happen because they are a byproduct of an environment and a mission that *desires good things to happen*. For example, running a successful business, providing healthcare services to the population, or promoting government engagement. Now place yourself in the role of a CIO who has to referee between supporting the sales executive, a powerful peer pushing for a technology-based enhancement that will drive sales growth, and the CISO, who is a direct report and who states categorically just how dangerous it would be to move forward.

Worse, the CISO is engaging in a chewed-up version of doom and gloom, like countless times before, and, as is usually the case, fails to propose any reasonable alternatives. To put the final nail in the coffin, the doom and gloom never actually seems to happen (and yes, I fully realize the missing word here is "yet"; bear with me, that's part of the point).

Is it any wonder that the CIO will, by and large, choose to go ahead with implementation?

The truly sad part is that by now, the folks practicing security in these common kinds of hierarchies have learned a valuable lesson: as long as fear is marketed powerfully enough, they can get extra resources approved. And the most dominant fear, at least in companies that have not yet suffered an actual breach with all of its glorious consequences, is the one driven by regulatory or industry compliance, like with the Payment Card Industry Data Security Standard (PCI-DSS). If there is ever a phrase that retail and hospitality executives will come to loath more than "PCI compliance," then surely it will involve devil worship. It is a stop button, a "you can't do business" button, a constant frustration that they are apparently powerless to overcome.

Welcome to the new motto in security: "management by compliance." We will discuss this tragic turn of events at length in Chapter 5.

Many security leaders behave as if saying no is their actual job. So here's an immediate lesson: as a CISO, you never want to say no. Ever. You want to advise and guide, surely, especially when you can offer unique insights. But you're not the *Department of No*. You're the *Department of How* (to do it safely).

Another big reason why security should not be managed within IT is even simpler: security problems are rarely, at their core, technology problems, even though they can *often be addressed with the assistance of technology*. Note that this is entirely different from saying that the problems originate with technology.

I realize the risk of making this statement. There is a sort of imagery, common in security circles, that implies their job is being the guard in front of the castle; that they must design the best moat and gate and mantrap and other surrounding defenses—in the form of technology infrastructure—to protect what's on the inside of the castle, which is sensitive company data. This visual, in many different forms, is reflected in countless security training and instruction manuals, videos, and other forms of education, and is accepted (or even assumed) by default. One of the earliest manufacturers of firewalls used, in the Nineties, a marketing slide evocative of this idea—the castle, the gate, the moat and the alligators, and the guard, with a firewall, at a keyboard. It was an easily understandable analogy for anyone listening, and it didn't hurt Checkpoint's fairly successful pursuit of world domination.

And yet, in this day and age, this approach is self-defeating, for two reasons.

The first reason is fetchingly described (at least if you like Mexican food) by my good friend and security expert, Steve Levinson, who likes to call it the "Hard Taco" problem—as in, crunchy shell, soft (and leaky) core. If you imagine the shell as your perimeter defenses and whatever is inside the taco as your data, the image becomes irresistible. It is also often discussed in the context of "defense in depth," which tends to be misunderstood just as often (and just as happily miscommunicated by security vendors) as simply a gated system of somewhat similar technology solutions. You might hear a security manager describing the "defense in depth" strategy as essentially a series of network-based firewalls and intrusion detection systems combined with network segmentation. That is akin to calling the enforcement of multiple password controls "multifactor authentication." Both are wrong (*multifactor* means different types of controls rather than multiples of the same control), but they are wrong in a nonintuitive way, thereby making the error harder to avoid.

The essential idea behind the castle and the alligators is that if we protect ourselves from the outside world, we will end up doing just fine. It's intuitive; after all, it's easy to think of the world in this "us versus them" fashion, with the bad guys (those dang hackers) on the outside knocking on the doors trying to get in, but the reality of security is quite different. *Internal and behavioral* threats can be far more devastating than external ones, and may materialize in many ways, such as social engineering, inadvertent leaks, bribery, employee disgruntlement, and even a simple lack of interest in security because "it is an IT problem." For an entertaining expose on this topic, please consider picking up my second book, *The Security Hippie*. Sadly, once somebody with malicious intent has access (they are past the crunchy shell), they will generally and easily be able to expand that access and get to the data (soft core). So many breaches in recent years illustrate this point (Twitter, anyone?) We will discuss this more in Chapter 6, but there is a question I like to ask executives locked in the "security in IT" mindset: "think back to 20 or 30 years ago, when all your sensitive stuff could be locked in safes and file cabinets. How many of your employees had access to those materials?" The answer is always a version of "very few," often accompanied by a nervous chuckle. And it is a telling chuckle because, in the modern age, with the promise of the paperless office in the here and now, they can't tell who can get to what and when, *not even if they ask*. But they do know one thing: the IT guy can access everything, and also controls who else has access. At least when a safe was physically broken into, you could tell immediately upon finding it that it happened (well, unless you're in one of those Le Carré novels, I suppose). Even that simple assumption isn't true in information security, where breaches are usually detected weeks, months, and sometimes even years after the fact, if they get detected at all.

The second reason is that security pros who emerge from the technology ranks are indeed incredibly smart, dedicated, and often selfless, for security is a thankless job. But there is another trait they usually share, which is a lack of business training and business operations experience. This lack of context leads to a tremendous disconnect, which makes sense: a very smart, highly technical person is asked to "protect the company," but is generally limited by their insight into how a company operates—things like business models and cashflows, sales and growth strategy—and instead, are buried in the IT hierarchy. Is it any wonder that they constantly seem to "miss the mark" and focus on the wrong things, while making endlessly dire predictions? Or that everything seems like a major threat to them? Worse, they know that if they screw up, it is their head that will roll before anybody else's.

Is it any wonder that these folks can come across as paranoid, unpleasant, or even scary?

As an aside, have you ever heard someone in security use the "I worry about the things I don't know that I don't know"? That's a losing game. Instead, my friend, realize that you're not in national security. Why don't you start worrying about the things you know that you don't know? What's your company's revenue model and profit margin? That "C" in your title means that yes, it is very much your business.

HOW SECURITY FIRMLY PLACES ITS FOOT IN ITS MOUTH IN THE MOST MUNDANE OF WAYS

A SHORT ESSAY ON A BORING TOPIC

Let's talk about passwords.

It's alright, go ahead. I will wait patiently for you to groan and roll your eyes.

You already know everything there is to know about passwords. They need to be long, and complex, and rotated frequently, and all that jazz. After all, that's what security professionals insist is the only way to keep anybody safe. Heck, even journalists seem to get it, and that's a seriously high bar to cross.

That this advice is generally wrong and is no more than a technological manifestation of a form of inertia is, well, not something we really want to discuss.

Or maybe you've evolved away from this. You're up to speed on passphrases. You know what two-channel authentication means, you know your SSO's and your revised NIST standards (took those guys long enough to get it, too).

Good for you.

Do you think passwords are a good authentication mechanism in general?

Because they aren't. They suck. It's just that they were the earliest form that we could easily implement in a client-server topology, and they stuck around since then. We're finally seeing the emergence of "passwordless authentication," but it's going to take a long time for something this embedded to truly shift.

Alright, alright, let's roll back for a minute here.

What on earth am I talking about?

Instead of trying to explain everything, let me give you an example—and a little quiz.

Ready?

Do you go to Starbucks?

We all do, right? Even if some of us only do it for dessert. I don't mean the actual dessert, but rather the sickeningly sweet dessert that pretends to be coffee. So . . . Do I get my honorary "Cranky" badge now? If not quite yet, then let me forever ruin my career (or help me launch one in standup comedy) by sharing my moniker of my favorite Starbucks concoction: a tall, blond, flat white, extra hot. I call it the *Trophy Wife*.

Anyway, back to our example.

Do you use the Starbucks mobile app?

If you don't yet, I recommend you try it, if only to avoid the lines. Plus it tracks all your stuff and gives you rewards. It's a well-designed app with a fairly friendly user interface (UI). Clearly, a lot of money and effort was invested in developing it, and some very good UI people were involved.

So what does that have to do with this book?

Let us now examine an area where Starbucks information security got involved. How do I know? Because they had to: it's the payment section. Security had to be involved, because it's a critical portion of the app that deals with sensitive consumer financial information—credit card accounts.

The way the app works to collect information about you, such as your favorite drinks, rewards, and behavior, is by assigning you an internal ID. Conveniently, you can enter a credit card into the app, and reload a certain amount onto your Starbucks profile in advance. You can even set the app to autoload more funds from your credit card to your Starbucks profile whenever your balance falls too low. Or you can reload it manually yourself.

And obviously, when you attempt to run a transaction this way, the app will ask for your password to ensure that it was you who issued the request.

Are we good so far?

No, really.

I mean it. Are we good so far?

If you were anticipating that I was about to make a point, you missed it, because the point was already made.

Can you tell where?

It's in the last sentence, about the need to enter your password. It is a classic example of an innocent, well-intentioned, security screwup.

How so?

It's easy to see when we think of it, not from a security controls perspective, but from a human behavioral perspective.

I'll ask a simple question: when would you typically be attempting to reload your card?

For most of us, it will be at exactly the least convenient time to do so—that is, while en route to or in line (or trying to avoid the line) at the store, while on your phone.

It's human nature. That's how we do.

So now the app is asking you to enter your password at the least convenient moment, when you are most hurried in its use. It's annoying to even have to think about it, but there it is. It's important to protect our credit card, after all.

Right?

So what is a loyal Starbucks customer to do?

You know the answer already. *You pick a simple password that's easy for you to remember.*

And there it is. A well-intentioned security control that is divorced from situational human behavior has resulted in a weakening of the *entire ecosystem* of the Starbucks e-commerce platform—because that same password is *also* used to login to the main Starbucks Web site, where a lot more personal information and transactional capabilities about Starbucks customers are available to the enterprising malicious collector of passwords.

There are many ways to solve this while making it easier for the end-users and strengthening the overall security of the ecosystem (biometrics, or the thankfully increasingly prevalent two-channel approach using an SMS code sent to the phone are two), but one thing is fairly clear: there was some form of disconnect at the business level between the security group and the folks who designed the UI.

It's exhibited via this transaction flow.

Don't get me wrong. I am not picking on Starbucks here. I'm just using it as an illustration of a frighteningly common problem, where security does its thing in a vacuum. And while the Starbucks app had evolved dramatically since I originally wrote this segment, and does attempt to utilize biometrics, it still asks me for the stupid password randomly when I try to add money to my rewards account. They have quite literally pushed me towards primarily ordering from Peet's instead.

Who, exactly, are they protecting?

To illustrate the prevalence of this problem, let's try another one. Time to pick on United Airlines, another well-known giant. Look at Figure 1.1.

This email arrived a couple of months before this book was originally written, and I found it so amusing that I had to capture it.

So, can you tell what the issue is?

It is basically a version of the same problem. Note the description in the first bullet: you would have to provide your password to the automated system when calling by phone. . . another example of a hidden inducement to pick a password that is easy to remember (and type in while, uh, driving).

And yet, it was supposedly designed this way in order to increase the security of the system!

When you extrapolate this at a large scale, you will easily see why "easy-to-remember" passwords are such an Internet scourge. And the sad part is that people are, effectively and indirectly, practically trained by security professionals to engage in unsafe practices, as these two examples among many, many others, show.

Worse, those same professionals then have the gall to blame people for poor password choices when their accounts inevitably get hacked.

It's not the users' fault.

It's our failure as a profession, a symptom of lazy thinking, a lack of interest to engage with our non-technical peers and the business itself that leads to this happening, over and over again.

MileagePlus # XXXXX336   **Barak, PINs are going away.**

Update about your MileagePlus PIN

To better protect your United MileagePlus® account, later this week, we'll no longer allow the use of PINs and implement two-factor authentication. This will impact you in two ways when accessing your MileagePlus account:

1. If you contact United® by phone, you'll be asked for your password when using the automated system or for your security answers when you speak to a United representative.
2. Your security questions will also be used as part of upcoming two-factor authentication to further protect your account—you'll be asked to answer your security questions the first time you sign in from a device that we don't recognize.

If you think you may have forgotten the answers to your security questions, we recommend that you <u>sign in</u> to your account and select new questions and answers now.

Thank you for being a MileagePlus member and for taking the time to update your account.

Learn more ›

Figure 1.1   Email received from United Airlines.

This is on us.

Before we get back to our regularly scheduled programming, here are a couple of tips to keep in mind with respect to passwords:

1   If passwords are a necessity, remember that length matters more than complexity. A string of 15 zeroes is more difficult to crack (using brute-force methods) than a fully randomized 8-character string, when both are properly hashed and salted.

2 Passwords are typically not a good way to deal with authorization, especially if the type of transaction involved is predetermined. Starbucks could have easily opted for an easier method of authorizing a reload within the mobile app using a challenge token (such as an SMS), because the worst that would happen would be that the user's credit card would fund that same user's Starbucks profile. The Peet's app, by the way, avoids this problem by not requiring a password to reload funds between previously added and approved payment methods. Considering when their app design changed, a part of me can't help but wonder if their security people read this book.

3 If you insist on using passwords, maybe due to technical reasons, then do yourself a favor and use different ones in different security contexts. The easiest method here is to, say, use a 4-digit PIN in low-security settings, and a password in high-security ones. And by all means, relax the complexity requirement and force length instead (see point 1), and while you're at it, please teach your users what a passphrase is.

4 Most importantly, please consider alternatives in the form of passwordless authentication. Most passwords are stolen, not cracked, with phishing being the most profitable venue for the thieves. If a password is stolen, it doesn't matter how well it's constructed.

This leads us to a third big reason why security is not a technology discipline, and it lies in the nature of the landscape that security professionals face. *Technical* security (operations) management is, by its very definition, a case of asymmetric warfare. It is a well-known reality that no security system is good enough to withstand all attacks, all the time. In the world of physical security, at least the cost of attack is higher; it will often involve some expenditure in equipment, maybe bribery and other techniques aimed at human compromise. There is also the risk of being caught, arrested, and punished. Both the attack and the response are essentially localized affairs.

In the world of digital security, the cost of attack is often minimal, detection rates are low, and legal and criminal prosecution is close to impossible due to cross-jurisdictional issues. Attacks can be distributed, coming in from all over the world including, lest we forget, the inside— even as the people executing them can physically be anywhere, and out of reach of the law. As such, a patient attacker has only to try enough times in order to be successful, because they only have to be right one time.

The poor schmuck . . . err, defender on the other side can't ever be wrong.

They literally have no chance.

That in itself can be quite depressing. But when reduced to the realm of technology management, it can feel downright fatalistic. There is never enough technology that one can buy to protect everything, but in a world where new attacks evolve much faster than the typical budget cycle, one apparently has to accept the reality that their job, career, and good name may be lost tomorrow, and there is pretty much nothing they can do about it.

And the fact is that most security managers, as we discussed earlier, have very little foundation to grasp what truly matters to the business due to lack of context. This is a great way to spread misery, and by now you can surely understand why I like to call information security the *Dismal Discipline*.

Is it any wonder that security managers often sleep so little, drink so much, and are the most cynical and least agreeable in the IT organization?

I think by this time you will agree that, just like in that definition of insanity, continuing to think about security as a technology problem even when that idea is clearly bunk, is tantamount to insanity.

The email comes through from a friend who is a recruiter. "Barak," he says, "I wonder if you could help me." The email goes on to say that one of his big clients has decided to seek a candidate for the newly created position of CISO, and is struggling to find the right candidate. He was wondering if it was a problem with the job description. It ends with "can you help tweak it please?" The current job description follows.

I skim through it, and find no surprises. It includes a list of hoped-for technology-related skills and expertise, some boilerplate about management experience, and a couple of desired educational credentials and certifications like a BSc in computer science and a CISSP. In fact, it reads pretty much like a typical director of IT security position, albeit with a fancified title.

"This reads like a fancified Director of IT Security position," I write back, and ask "What are they really looking for?"

He gets back to me right away. "Yeah, I know. They don't know exactly what they want, except that the last guy who had the director role left unhappy. That's why I am asking you for help."

I call him. In a depressingly familiar conversation, I learn that the company feels that security is important—the board and the top executives read the news, breaches are scary, and they don't want to be the next name in the headlines—and even though they have tried doing something about it, their experience has been somewhat disappointing. Nobody ever understood the guy running security, who communicated badly and kept spending money on "who knows what," reassuring them that "everything was going to be fine," while at the same time fostering a sense of urgency by adding, "if only we buy more security tools immediately." Needless to say, nobody felt reassured, but they were all a little afraid of him, and of the news, and so he kept getting his way. What really threw them off, though, was that he never seemed happy—it was hard to believe everything really was fine when the person telling you that everything was alright constantly appeared constipated while saying it.

I have seen this play out countless times, in different organizations of different sizes in different verticals. Even where the understanding of security as a risk management discipline—a critical insight— was practically built into the culture, like in large banks, often the implementation of that insight was lacking, although in somewhat differing ways.

Plus considering the harshness of the grind, security people really suck at celebrating success.

As a result, companies repeatedly and recurrently *hire wrong*. They will hire smart, experienced people, and then set them up to fail. Or they will hire not-so-great but confident-seeming people, and let them "do their thing," which does little to improve the security posture, but does a lot to introduce self-serving processes, at a significant human resource cost.

More about these last two points in the add-on chapter, next.

Here are common thought processes that lead to this pattern, and a response to each one:

- *Claim*: Security is hard.
- *The truth*: Security is no harder than managing cashflows or penetrating new markets. All are disciplines that require a particular expertise. It just so happens that information security, at present, is evolving rapidly and has a lower number of established leaders because it hasn't been around for as long. That doesn't make it harder. Being a CISO is just as difficult (or as easy) as being a CIO or CTO.

  There is another element at play here, which is the good ol' profit motive. The security space is filled with vendors offering niche solutions, using FUD (fear, uncertainty, and doubt) and fantastical claims that only serve to keep security unapproachable. We've been here before with technology. Yes, the Nineties, I'm looking at you.

- *Claim*: Security is a higher stakes game.
- *The truth*: A favorite statement of candidates to the position of CISO, this is not only wrong, but dangerous. So let's set this one straight. Security is there to *support the business* in its highest stakes game—in the case of a for-profit enterprise, manufacturing product, obtaining and serving customers, and carving out market share. A security person who is focused on technology threats all day will never be able to properly analyze the risk inherent in everyday business decisions, and will likely become ever more conservative in their decision making. The end result? The company pays lip service to the security leader while ignoring them where it really matters. This in turn leads them to become even more paranoid, frustrated, and upset, which in turn drives everyone else to behave even more

covertly so as not to piss them off . . . until it all breaks down, they quit (or get fired), and a new person comes on-board to start the cycle anew (I'll share a story about this shortly). In the meantime, processes do fail and the business ends up assuming more risk than necessary, because everyone is afraid of bringing in the security person for important decisions, since they always slow things down significantly. Sometimes that can lead to a bad data leak, which can harm the brand. At this point, when asked for my opinion, I tend to dismiss the candidacy of any security practitioner for the role of CISO who uses the "higher stakes" argument.

- *Claim*: Security is a technology problem and can be solved with technology.

- *The truth*: We just spent a few pages discussing this issue, so hopefully we are on the same page by now. I do want to add a thought here, though. For the purpose of this discussion, I will assume you provide some sort of service or product that directly targets consumers or businesses—a b2c or b2b (or b2b2c) type environment. Ask your prospective CISO who their most important partnership is with, outside of their boss or direct reports. There are the typical answers—CIO, CTO, VP Engineering or Operations, and so on. Some go further and mention the CFO or Chief Counsel, which shows a deeper understanding of the role. But the best ones will say "everyone," and mention the heads of sales and marketing. We will explore later why these are such important business partners to the security leader, and hopefully, your candidate will be able to do the same, and give you concrete examples as to how this partnership has worked for them successfully in the past.

- *Claim*: If we aren't compliant, we'll have to shut down our doors.

- If you haven't heard that one, and you're a senior executive in any reasonably sized enterprise, then you are either (1) woefully behind the fear curve or (2) lucky to have a real security pro. If it's the latter, I congratulate you. If it's the former, please reach out to me, I can help. But most likely, you have heard it before. The truth is that even in places where draconian security measures are enforced—say, the NSA—there is almost always wiggle room even after things go bad. Yes, there is an exception that proves the rule; one is Card Systems International, which eventually shut down after a massive 2005 breach due to the aggregate damages claims from their business customers, not any regulator. But for the most part, companies can and do survive breaches. This is not to discount the heavy cost of breaches, in both remediation costs as well as ongoing costs for years, and in particular, a burden placed on technology use that can have a direct impact on the company's ability to grow. But using this kind of language isn't helping anyone. Did it ever really convince you, deep down? Or if you said it, did you ever truly believe it? Or were you using it to get your way?

All of these—and other—surprisingly common misconceptions about security drive toward one outcome, which is a series of failed security leadership hires.

Instead, I would suggest that companies reconsider the role of CISO in a different light. A fair number of books and articles have been written on the practice of security as risk management. They would be right, with an important caveat: information security is about managing *business risk related to the use of technology*, rather than technology risk directly. In this sense, the CISO is akin to the risk manager in a trading firm—they (should) have the enormous power to stop business from happening, but it is a power they must learn to use very judiciously (hopefully never), or else they will become ridiculed by other business leaders, and worse, ignored and overridden regularly in the decision-making process, even when they are completely in the right.

I would like, however, to take it one step further, and suggest that the CISO should be thought of as a business enabler. This was not always true, but as technology has become pervasive in every part of the business, it brings with it both tremendous risk and tremendous opportunity. The right kind of CISO can serve as a bridge between the needs of the business and the risks related to the use of technology in supporting those needs. It's just like the CIO who is translating those same business needs into applied technology to support those needs.

This may superficially seem to contradict my statement that security is not a technology discipline. But it is not so. A good security leader does not need to understand the nitty-gritty of the technologies in use, just like the CIO does not need to know how to configure the email system. The CIO brings value in the strategic sense of how to most effectively direct technology where its value is truly realized; the CISO fills a similar role in terms of risk.

But because the CISO understands those risks in a way that may be different from the rest of the executive team, they can suggest opportunities to use technology—and information—in a way that could trigger new and profitable avenues for the business to pursue, without adding risk. Their training and ability to balance risk and reward, and their proximity (if placed appropriately within the company structure) to the "piping" of the company, gives them this opportunity. Viewed this way, the CISO is an advisor to the business, rather than a technology savant.

As an example, I will bring up the case of a transactional platform company serving the retail vertical. This was when technologies like Web application firewalls (WAFs) were first coming to market, and were considered bleeding-edge. In working with the company's business leaders and looking for a way to gain a competitive edge, we made the case that by adding this technology to the company's offerings, we could attain three significant benefits: (a) we would dramatically enhance the security posture of the organization in a world where threats were evolving ever more rapidly; (b) with proper messaging, we could significantly enhance the company's trust messaging in the marketplace; and (c) we would "future-proof" the company's compliance posture, since compliance standards (in this case, PCI-DSS) were bound to catch up. Oh, and then there was (d) we would repackage this service as a premium add-on, allowing the company to *recoup its investment and turn a small profit.*

And it worked.

Of course, there was risk involved. Justifying an expenditure of this magnitude at the time was hard. But by collaborating with sales and marketing to test the waters with strategic customers, we were able to do it, and gain all those benefits. But do you notice one thing missing from the above description? There is no discussion of "what would happen if we didn't." No FUD was necessary. It was a case of security and business leadership coming together to examine a security-initiated business proposal, and accept it as good for the business and a potential growth driver.

Certainly, we gained a nice side effect of protecting technology assets.

Unfortunately, this is rarely the case. In fact, the most common "methodology" (if you will) for managing information security these days is compliance targets. Retail and hospitality are indeed verticals where this is particularly pronounced, with PCI often dictating security decisions; if it's not in scope for PCI and the company can pass its audit without it . . . well, good luck getting funding. But it's not just in retail and hospitality anymore. The PCI standard itself has now transitioned across boundaries to many other industries that are only peripherally involved with credit cards. Retailers, after all, have many vendors, and it has become standard practice to require PCI compliance documentation before services can be acquired. Healthcare organizations are, naturally, focused on security requirements in HIPAA. Banks, of course, have many regulations to contend with (and have settled on SOC2 as a common measure of trustworthiness). Companies with European presence or dealing with EU residents must adhere to European privacy regulations (such as the General Data Protection Regulation [GDPR]) or face the risk of fines of up to 4% of their global revenue. And so on.

At this point, one might legitimately ask the following question: why is this bad? After all, increased data protection regulation, often coupled with increased scrutiny, can only be a good thing, right? It holds companies accountable.

And the answer is, certainly, it should. But it pretty much never works that way.

But for now, let's focus our attention on the security leader's business role.

Uncomfortable truth: If someone wants you bad enough, they will get you. Why do we insist on giving people an impossible job that will get them fired when they inevitably fail?

1.2
A Case Study

Welcome to the second edition!

To make it easiest to read if you've read the book before, I am placing most of the new content in these sub-chapters. They are also denoted with a ".2" which seemed a nice way to make everything extra clear.

Anyway, before I proceed, I'd like to share a favorite Frank Herbert quote (that's the guy who wrote Dune): *The undeserving maintain power by promoting hysteria.*

I don't think I need to explain how this is contextually relevant, do I? Didn't think so.

But I did want to share a story with you, as a point of illustration. Think of it as a case study for misbehaving CISOs.

The company was a fairly big one—over a thousand employees, gorilla-in-its-market sort of status, known and respected brand, IPO forthcoming . . . you know the drill.

Then one of their board members reaches out to me. He knows me from some other things we'd done together, and asks if I would be willing to help them. He's an important figure in Silicon Valley, and sits on a lot of technology boards.

"You see," he says, "they have this CISO guy." I recognize that most of my stories start this way. I can't help it.

He goes on.

"They like him. He's trusted, and he's had good relationships with most of the senior staff and even with us on the board." Well, that's an unusual twist, so I make sure to tune in carefully. "But he just quit, and he threw a bomb when he did, and I'm not sure what to make of it. Would you consider assessing the situation and giving us your opinion?"

Yes, it was pretty much a rhetorical question, but I appreciated it anyway.

Introductions are made, and I get to know the players and the story.

Upon leaving, the prior CISO sent an explicit email that, in terms that I can only refer to as downright frightening, made it clear that the company was doing security so badly that it was acting in a borderline fraudulent fashion. He focused his accusations on the head of engineering, who he called incompetent, an idiot, and much, much worse. He used language that made it clear he considered it the end of the line; he had to quit or otherwise he'd have to notify "the regulator" of these terrible violations. He sent the letter to the board, and offered them continuing support as they "cleaned house" and fixed the problem.

Note that this was a private company, with no regulator in its space, so it certainly was an interesting claim to make. That aside, this was certainly an intriguing premise.

I spent a bit of time trying to unpack the security claims, including by interviewing the guy. He is very likeable, eloquent, smart and persuasive. He laid out his claims in a thoughtful manner, and if you didn't know any better, I bet you, too, would be scared out of your mind.

The thing is, I do know better, and the problem was with the substance.

There really wasn't any.

Sure, the company sucked at things like patch and vulnerability management, but not more so than comparable companies of its size and nature. This I could say with confidence, due to my own unique background in owning the security program in so many companies; the contextual comparison is second nature and automatic.

In fact, when I had the conversation with chief counsel before the engagement, I told him that, before I even saw the letter or interviewed anybody, I'd write down a short email describing what I thought those concerns might be, and vault it; we could check it after I was done to see how close I was to the truth.

Three months later, it turned out I was spot on in every single item, but I did miss a very big one that the CISO didn't mention, which was the most impactful to the organization; I'll get to it in a bit.

His biggest claim was around the company's use of embedded third-party software that was already end-of-life, and had a fair number of serious security vulnerabilities. He stated that the risk was so great that the company faced impending doom, and that the head of engineering refused to do anything about it. Now, don't get me wrong, this is a (very) bad practice, but it's not unusual. Plenty of engineering teams really suck at managing their third-party software, whether it's open-source libraries or previously acquired binaries.

In our conversation, he admitted that he knew that these problems were common, so I challenged him to explain his statement about being fraudulent. "Well, they know about it and won't do anything," he responded. I pointed out that, if it's a common issue in the industry, then it's hardly malicious, and arguably not even negligent; if everybody's doing it, then they are simply conforming to industry standard.

Eventually, he got to Joe Sullivan (whose case had not been resolved yet at that time). I discuss the case of Uber's CISO in a subsequent chapter, but it came down to this CISO being afraid that if he didn't notify someone, he'd end up in jail. That I could understand, misguided as it was; at least it gave a plausible motive for his explosive action. I tried to explain the arguably fairly significant difference between lying to a regulator about an actual breach while under investigation, and not doing a great job at patching systems, but it fell on deaf ears.

He was spooked.

Now that I had obtained his perspective, I could speak to the internal parties. I'm sure this wouldn't come as a shock to you, but the head of engineering was certainly not incompetent, and while she never had experience at that level, she was certainly learning quickly and adapting. She was even quite sympathetic to the issues that were raised in the letter, and acknowledged that it was an issue they were working to resolve—it just wasn't as simple as a "tear-and-replace" due to the architecture of their monolithic environment.

Read: it's complicated.

While I wasn't there to do CISO things, rather only as an advisor, I proposed my classic solution to this problem, which has been implemented to great satisfaction in countless engineering shops: instead of tackling the big problem, just tell all the engineers that the next time they release a code branch, that branch has to have updated software. Eventually, the problem will work itself out of the system (and they will have acquired a useful habit). It might take 18 months, but it will be done with minimum pain. She liked this and implemented it and from what I was told a year later, the old software was already gone, so they did even better than I would have thought.

They even started down the path towards a private bug bounty program.

So, you know, not exactly an indictment of anybody's skills or leadership.

When I concluded my assessment and presented it to the board, I felt more like a therapist than a security expert, at least in terms of the claims made in that scary letter.

But then I had to share the findings I made that I didn't expect.

And it was doozy.

Let me back up for a moment. When I shared my findings with chief counsel, I told him that while I didn't find anything particularly wrong with security operations, or at least not more wrong than I had expected to find in the first place. People suck at security all over the place, and they weren't any different.

But I did develop an unusual suspicion.

"Oh?" he asked.

"It's only a hunch, because it's not something I can prove, but . . . ." I hesitated.

"Go on," he prodded me.

"I think you have a shadow IT organization," I stated.

I went on to explain that, as I was speaking to various parties, it seemed like some of them—all closely associated with the CISO who had just left—were more loyal to the cause than loyal to the company. So much so that they viewed it as their duty to covertly disrupt internal operations until the company "fixed its shit."

A form of Italian Strike.

I'd seen it before, and so when the pattern emerged, it rang a bell. The CISO was charismatic, influential, and loyal to his people, and they paid him back in kind. He convinced them that the greatest service they could perform for the company was to expose engineering leadership as incompetent and malicious.

I named the few folks I thought were involved, in order of confidence, and reminded counsel that, again, this was just a hunch, and not anything I could back with fact. "Truth is," I added, "I haven't even spoken directly to a couple of them. It's just a vibe I picked up from various other conversations."

He was shocked.

Then he went on to say that the list of names I shared with him was a 1-for-1 match for his own list that he had been preparing for months, of people that were "problematic." He just couldn't quite place his finger on what made them so, until I suggested the shadow org concept. Then it all clicked. "And," he added, "you'd be amazed to know that after the CISO's departure, they have slowly been self-selecting out of the company". He shook his head. "I just don't understand how you did that from just a few chats with us."

I admitted that I didn't know either.

When I later presented to the board, they were both relieved and, when I spoke of the shadow org, taken aback. But the material resonated, and as all the loose ends clicked into place, they were grateful. "After all," my VC guy told me later, "we were afraid that we would lose tens of millions of investment dollars because the CISO made it sound like the whole thing had to be scrapped." He paused when he saw the question mark on my face. "Yes, Barak, for real. That's how scared we were."

Which is when Frank Herbert's words popped to my mind.

Not that this CISO was anything special in his approach. It is sadly likely that most of the folks who practice this discipline would tend to sympathize with him. I don't, clearly, but I'm also clearly in the minority.

Maybe you shouldn't listen to me?

There are many other areas where this kind of fear mongering is used regularly by security pros to needlessly waste enormous amounts of resources. I'd like to finish this chapter by discussing one of them: Third Party Risk Management.

We do way, way too much of it for no discernible business benefit.

I'll pause here to allow everyone to sharpen their knives, as I am clearly out of my mind.

Ready?

Here is how the story typically goes:

"We share our sensitive data with a lot of cloud vendors, and thus they present a risk to our data."

This statement is certified platinum.

"In order to minimize the risk to our data present by these vendors, we need to ensure that they can handle it safely."

This statement is also true, but it includes a sneaky word that carries an enormous emotional weight, which is immediately used to take a 90-degree detour into La-la Land.

Do you see it?

The word is "ensure."

We'll get back to this in a second, but let's take that detour first.

"If we don't do this, then when the *bad stuff* happens, we will [XXX]!" The X's here represent a host of really scary outcomes, from being sued to oblivion to shutting down the company to ending up in jail, getting divorced and having to euthanize your cat.

"And the only way to do this right . . ." Finally, having departed reality, we get to the crux of our fantastical tale. The demands—sorry, asks—here all sound reasonable: things like a team to handle sending out extensive requests for information (RFI, RFP, RFQ . . . should we just call them RFx?) with hundreds of questions about security, and then checking them when they come back, running all sorts of technical evaluations (like vulnerability scans and pentests) against the vendor, and a myriad of other activities that will "ensure" that the vendor handles your data securely.

Notice how the word "ensure" in this context targets fear.

Fear is the great motivator.

Before I tear this entire fictional structure apart, let me ask you: considering all the published breaches, let alone the ones we don't know about, by some of the biggest (and many smaller) tech names in the industry that handle a lot of large enterprise data for companies with entire teams dedicated to "ensuring" safety . . . how, uhh, *ensured* do you feel about how all of this is working out for everybody?

Trust me, companies like Segment and Windriver and Lastpass and Twilio—the list is endless—were subject to all of this scrutiny, too. Did all of this activity somehow stop the breaches? no. Did it even prevent a single customer from buying any of those services? Oh, of course not. What made them successful was their excellent product offerings and go-to-market strategy, not their security. Did this meaningless activity (in terms of measurable outcomes) waste a lot of time and annoy the hell out of both the buyers at their customers, and the vendors themselves, as they all twisted themselves into kinky shapes to satisfy the big bad CISOs who were driving all this nonsense?

You betcha.

"You're just *not doing it well enough*," is a response I often hear when I state this.

Right. Of course. Let's double down, then, and hire even more people to do even more absurd things for *ensurance* (you say "reassurance," I invent a new word. *Tomato, Tomahto*).

Where's that definition of insanity again?

Look, folks. I've been in this business a long time, and I dare anyone to prove that all this nonsense leads to a *consistent, measurable, material* improvement in *commercial outcomes* for the people engaged in all this activity—over, say, the simple proposition of requiring, asking for, and reviewing annually third-party audit reports, like the now wildly common SOC2 type-2, of those vendors.

Isn't this why we're supposedly doing this, after all? Protecting our for-profit commercial organization from negative commercial outcomes?

Remember, also, that all the money you're spending on these precious exercises doesn't come from nowhere. There is a limited amount of money to spend, and if you need to grow your market or protect your turf, innovation or (trigger word incoming!) *marketing* may be a better place to spend it.

Security leaders, understand this: you don't ever get to manage your vendors' security program, no matter how scary your countenance. They will answer your questions in a reasonable fashion that allows them to get through your boot camp exercise to sell you their services and products, and your own business buyer to sign the bottom line.

Not that you could stop your buyers anyway. That's because of one simple reason: they are in charge of important stuff, like moving the business forward. And in the places where you do stop them, they will sadly inform anyone in their orbit—vendors included—about how you, their security leader, are harming their ability to do business, hurting their competitiveness and the success of their organization.

To address the other common objection to this argument: if you think that this will somehow allow you to chase your vendors for more money in damages if something goes bad than the commercial liability agreed upon in the contract, you don't understand contract law. Not that you should—you're not a lawyer—but in my humble opinion, an intro course into contract law needs to be mandated for every prospective CISO.

Or get a damn MBA.

Hey, look, I just gave you an actionable recommendation!

Assuming your vendors already undergo regular security auditing and testing, which you would know from those audit reports, all that extra activity to "ensure" their security won't gain you a thing, and will lose you a fair bit. Sure, they might fix some point-in-time finding a couple of weeks earlier than they otherwise would have to close the deal with you, or at least pretend that they did something like that to grease the relationship.

Way to go, kid.

A gold star will be applied to your next pay check.

More on this topic as well as the grander one of overdoing things in security later, from different perspectives. And we will wrap it all up in the end, when we discuss a new paradigm for thinking about security management.

For now, just keep in mind that *hysteria* pretty much never leads to *good decision making*.

2

THE BUSINESS OF BEING CISO

The office of the CIO is large—one of the largest I've ever seen. The couch on which I am sitting is comfortable enough to sleep in. The view outside the window is impressive, and somewhat distracting. We've been here for a little while discussing why, in particular, this Fortune-500 executive should bother with bringing me on as a consultant to help with, of all things, enterprise security. And we're talking because the case being made is that the help is needed, not necessarily on a technical or operational level, but in terms of the company's business strategy.

In other words, I'm not here to configure firewalls.

It's actually going surprisingly well, even though I am admittedly somewhat intimidated. I only incorporated my "company" earlier that year, after a few years of operating under my individual banner. The custom-tailored suit I'm wearing is the most expensive article of clothing I have ever owned, which is good, but my shoes in this company show their off-the-shelf origin, and it shows.

For heaven's sake, why am I thinking about my shoes? Concentrate, Barak!

I have already decided that no matter what happens, the CIO is one of my favorite people ever. Gregarious, smart, witty—I can't help but like him as we go through an increasingly uncomfortable vivisection of my career experiences and the reasoning behind why he should allocate a budget to this effort, then rapidly switching to favorite war stories, clearly a trust-building experience.

There's a pause in the conversation.

DOI: 10.1201/9781003302759-4

"OK, Barak. So just tell me one thing," he switches gears. I tense up. My brain goes on alert. He looks directly at me, with a smile, but do I detect a glint in his eye?

"Why are you so expensive?"

Truth is, I'm not. I know that. In fact, I've before charged twice, in terms of hourly rates, what is in this proposal. I know he's testing me. This is not a real question—it's a validation exercise, a device designed to assess my handling of it, regardless of the content. During later years, I came to learn that he would often ask these sorts of off-the-wall questions, just to see how someone would respond, and gauge their reaction. It helped him judge their character.

My sense is that how I answer may determine the fate of our relationship.

I take an uncomfortably long, 2-second break to consider. Then it comes to me, and I retort with what is, admittedly, a bit of relish.

"Because I'm Jewish."

The room seems to rock slightly as we laugh ourselves into initialing the contract.

Let me go old style on you for a moment.

Roughly three decades ago, the notion of a paperless office came forcefully into being, as well as common definition. In some ways, it was the first truly significant "computer revolution," in that it entered the common person's technology awareness as a way of efficiently running a business. With advances in computing and networks, it seemed that in just a few short years, companies would no longer need to depend on paper (soon to be joined by desk phones, mail, and other stone-age relics) at all. It made sense, but the resulting cycle fit the classic technology hype cycle to a "T"; it took many more years than predicted to get there, and when it finally did happen, nobody seemed to notice. The transition turned out to be almost too gradual (Figure 2.1).

Yet happen it did.

Eventually.

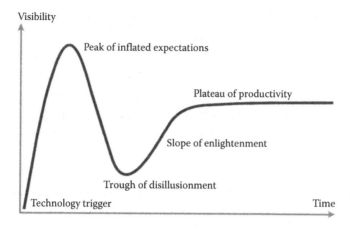

Figure 2.1   Gartner research's hype cycle diagram. (From Jeremykemp at English Wikipedia, https://commons.wikimedia.org/wiki/File:Gartner_Hype_Cycle. svg; Gartner Hype Cycle, https://crea tivecommons.org/licenses/by- sa/3.0/legalcode.)

Today, of course, we live in a reality where the enterprise is, indeed, living "in the network," whether it is local and portable (the CEO's laptop and mobile devices), localized (the office networked file system), co-hosted in some data center usually belonging to somebody else, or (increasingly) virtually in the cloud. Today's big advances that aim to disrupt and enhance the mechanisms of business creation and growth are the cloud, big data analytics, mobile computing including BYOD (bring your own device, also known as the bane of IT departments everywhere), and Internet of Things (IoT)—a term which is set to become the number one term used in security product marketing in 2017. (Note from the 2nd edition future: this prediction played out pretty much as, well, predicted).

Whereas in that incredibly distant past of the late twentieth century, a top executive could limit access to sensitive information simply by locking it in their office safe, thereby also guaranteeing, more-or-less, that unauthorized access is at least pretty noticeable, today they must rely on an army of people (the IT folks) to manage a kind of digital safe whose keys are not even in that executive's pocket. The CEO can access the safe just like anybody else. The keys are in the IT department.

And not only are those keys not physical (passwords aside), but they are also often practically impossible to imagine if you're not a technie.

Don't believe me? Alright. Please describe an encryption key . . . in relatable, easy-to-understand layman's terms. I'll wait.

Heck, when examining security policy, I always find myself having to mentally shake off the cobwebs when inserting clauses related to locking away sensitive documents . . . mostly because many new companies often don't even have locks on internal doors, let alone safes or even heavy furniture in which to lock stuff—all previously popular policy terms.

Worse, our modern executive has to make a lot of other assumptions, which if they are smart (most executives did not get to that position by being stupid) they know are complete bunk. They are expected to trust that the IT department will set up access in a way that reflects a proper and nuanced understanding of current business requirements behind granting such access to particular individuals; react in real time to shifts in business environment that IT has no visibility into nor the experience to interpret in any contextual sense; ensure that this virtual safe is properly guarded at all times; and so on. I won't even go into special business scenarios, such as the surreptitious changing of the safe code due to a suspicion that an insider may have been able to gain access to it in order to make copies of documents to take with them to their new employer, which happens to be a direct competitor.

I can go on, but you get the point. Any sane person in senior management knows, with unshakable confidence, that as much as they *adore* and *trust* their IT administrators, there is no way they can expect them to make the right access decisions, day in and day out, to critical data. It is a source of continuing tension between the business leaders—CEO, COO, CFO—and their company's technology hierarchy.

This helps explain the emergence in those olden days of the CIO as a force in the executive committee. A good CIO will translate business requirements into technology solutions, hopefully implement them in trustworthy fashion, and, by virtue of being at the table, be able to do so on an ongoing basis. They serve as a bridge between the business and the dark, geeky forces that lubricate its machinery. It also, handily, gives the CIO a forward career path, perfectly illustrated in the trajectory of a long-time customer of mine who went from VP of IT to CIO to COO and subsequently President of his Fortune-500 firm.

But a good CIO is there to provide functionality, to translate changing business requirements into technology decisions. Their risk view, by the very nature of their highly demanding role, is driven by questions such as "how do I make this happen cheaper/better/faster?" and "what sort of things are out there that can help me with making it easier for the business to grow?"

These are critical questions, and they deserve the CIO's full attention. Thus, except in a general sense around efficiency and reliability, they are not typically in the business of assessing indirect risks to the business inherent in such usage or, for that matter, *lack of* usage.

Which is where the CISO comes in.

In many ways, today's CISO finds themselves in a position not dissimilar to that of the CIO in the roarin' '90s. As discussed earlier, they are often technologically minded, sitting as it were in the eye of a gathering storm, and thrust with a major responsibility from multiple sources that often appear to be in conflict with each other. Worse, the CISO often has to interpret these conflicting demands without the appropriate business training or background, which inevitably leads to either a highly conservative or highly risky decision-making process, and often both, depending on their personality and the issue at hand.

How many times have you heard a variation of the following questions and statements in the context of a security conversation?

"Are we compliant?"

"Are our systems secure?"

"This deal has to close by Friday, we have to do it."

"If we don't do this, we won't be in business any more, so figure it out."

The problem with these kinds of statements is that they are anchored in a lot of hidden, assumed context. For example, the question "are we compliant?" means different things when asked by a sales VP, a CTO, or a general counsel. The first is interested in whether it is possible to produce the necessary reassurance to prospects in a manner that would be acceptable and remove sales barriers; the second in the level of technology (and technology implementation) adherence to a given standard; the third in whether any liability (business or personal) is present. It only takes a simple misunderstanding of the specific context of the conversation to lead to significant friction down the road.

Even more interestingly, it is entirely possible that the answer is legitimately different in each of these contexts, even if the underlying reality is the same!

For example, the following answers may *all be true at the same time*. *Question: Are we compliant? (with some standard, rule, or regulation)*

- Answer (to the VP of Sales): Yes!
- There is a current audit document validating compliance that can be shared with a prospect.
- Answer (to the CTO): No!
- There are certain known deficiencies that were not shared with, understood, or discovered by the auditor, but are known internally to the team.
- Answer (to the general counsel): Maybe?
- The interplay between the existing contractual commitment and the known current security posture may leave an unknown liability on the books, depending on the interpretation of negligence and the specific statements made and artifacts included related to information security in the contract.

Lacking the proper business background and operational context, it will be very difficult to reconcile these positions without frustrating the various audiences. The path from here to losing credibility is rather short.

The modern CISO also has to contend with another challenge, which is the extended sphere of (data) control. In the past, information was fairly easily contained—even in electronic form, it was typically on company-owned servers in company-controlled co-hosted cages or data centers. But the rapid emergence of cloud computing has changed all that. Even the most paranoid organization tends to rely on a fair number of such services, such as (say) Netsuite and Salesforce for business and customer relationship management (CRM), and the improved technical operational efficiency inherent in cloud services is tempting an increasing number of companies to move all of their backoffice functionality to the cloud.

Then you add remote connectivity, any number of employee-owned end-user devices (hello, smart phones!), and the idea that company data has boundaries quickly becomes mostly pretense. If you're lucky, you can track access to stuff you really care about, but even that is debatable. After all, it's hard to ever tell whose fingers are actually typing behind the screen, and it's already possible to ask your fridge to read your corporate emails aloud to you.

Such expansion, while terrific for the IT department's ability to successfully master and scale ever-more complex business needs and environments, can introduce many headaches to the security organization. Not only is data now stored and handled elsewhere, it is often nigh impossible to draw clear boundaries, not just around the data itself, but also between the various management responsibilities of the associated infrastructures, which in themselves are virtual and rather abstract.

In our practice, we see this all the time, especially when we work with cloud-based service providers. Take, for example, the issue of the "invisible NOC."

Say again? What is that?

The invisible NOC (Network Operations Center) is composed of the personnel at the cloud company—say, Amazon—who manage the underlying cloud infrastructure and in particular, the virtualization infrastructure. Let's focus on those folks that have access to the hypervisors, those central management components that drive all virtual environments, allocate available resources, and otherwise allow the concept of virtual computing to exist at scale.

Why do they matter so much?

Well, if you have access to the hypervisors, then you have access to anything those hypervisors manage, with no limit and no accountability. Or at least not to the supposed downstream owner of the virtual machines themselves.

You know, the cloud customers.

This is, if you will, a known level of abstraction. As a cloud customer, you are never fully in control of your own virtual devices and whatever you place on or transition through them. Don't think encryption protects you, because the people running the infrastructure can always see keys in memory if they so choose. You must assume that the cloud provider hires trustworthy personnel to fill these technical operations positions, that they have proper controls and auditing mechanisms to catch them if they make mistakes or go rogue, processes for handling such behaviors and notifying you if something bad happens, and so on and so forth. This is not a new concept: your telecommunications provider (say, AT&T) controls the piping through which you send your data, and the devices that enable it on each end. Generally speaking, they could easily read anything you sent through them, but we trust them not to do so.

To go back to the public cloud, and while I realize that I will bring down the wrath of many with the following statement, it is fair to suggest that the NOCs of the big cloud providers (Amazon, Google, Microsoft) are the best in the business, simply by virtue of them being able to operate successfully for so long on such a massive scale. Proof is in the proverbial pudding.

But the truth is, you never really know, the cloud provider's terms and conditions are typically identical for all cloud customers, and (as a matter of law) companies are generally not criminally liable for criminal acts undertaken independently by their employees. The rest is just umbrella liability.

Now let's go back to our hypothetical cloud-based SaaS (software-as-a-service) provider. They have decided, sensibly, that their real value lies in the application they provide, rather than the associated data center operations. They elect to rent their computing infrastructures from a cloud provider—let's assume one of the big three, Amazon AWS, Google GCP, or Microsoft Azure.

This allows them to do a lot of neat tricks, like spin up fully functional, highly scalable software quickly, and add bells and whistles rapidly as well. They can even spin up their platform directly from fresh code, a concept known as "platform as software," often from a well-known cloud-based software management repository; by far the most popular, GitHub, is owned by Microsoft. Used properly, all of this abstraction can reduce deployment cycles and recovery times dramatically.

Thus, this SaaS vendor, even if they are themselves very small, can make their offering very tempting to the enterprise customer who is looking to solve big, often legacy problems. So they attract such customers fairly early on in their business cycle, and inevitably, at some point in the acquisition cycle, the enterprise customer's security team must get involved.

Here is what typically happens next.

That enterprise security team has to validate and verify hundreds of vendors at any given time. The enterprise (or agency) CISO must find a way to balance the risks inherent in vendor management with the business (and regulatory) requirements driving these new vendor requests. As we discussed earlier, they are generally incentivized to err on the side of caution; after all, if a vendor screws up, it will be the enterprise CISO who could get canned for "failing to properly review" that vendor in advance.

So a standardized process is created to support vendor risk validation. The folks tasked with creating it usually have even less business context than the CISO (who often doesn't have it either), and are even more enthusiastic in their efforts to create a "comprehensive process" for validating vendors.

Then legal gets involved, and requirements continue to grow.

You get the picture. By the time everybody is satisfied that the process is robust, it has grown to take the form of multiple (and often contextually ridiculous) contractual clauses and a 600-question RFx that makes roughly seven million (give or take a few) generalized assumptions about technology vendors that are often quite removed from reality—especially for SaaS providers.

The kicker is when these documents are intended to be embedded in the contract, and become contractual artifacts with legal, binding force.

The service provider—in many cases, a rapidly growing startup, often with only a handful of employees and barebones backoffice operations—now has to somehow answer these questions and finds that the other side is not very attentive to their pleas for sanity. They must attest to physical controls for environments that they do not manage, nor have any visibility into (the cloud company's data centers). They must contractually grant their enterprise customer a right to audit their data processing facilities, for an environment they cannot access themselves, thereby breaking the contract by the simple act of signing it. They must agree to personnel drug screening requirements that are entirely inappropriate and counterculture for their business. And the list goes on.

But do you know what never seems to bother the enterprise customer? In all of these questions, surveys, attestations, contractual requirements, and so on, no one ever mentions the invisible NOC—a group of practically invisible people which the SaaS vendor relies on but has no ability to monitor.

Isn't it fascinating?

Of course, in the context of business liability, the enterprise counsel's answer to that is "the cloud provider is represented by the SaaS vendor." Good luck with that line when the cloud gets broken and all you have as a remedy are the very limited resources, warranties, and embarrassingly small (if any) cyber-insurance coverage of that vendor.

They'll probably go bankrupt first.

A small number of enterprises have enlightened security leaders that understand this and take a different route. They independently review and accept certain cloud vendors every year, and then have a shortened approval process for cloud-based service providers that are located inside those clouds. For example, an enterprise may "pre-accept" AWS with a dedicated VPC (virtual private cloud) as a cloud infrastructure, allowing any service provider using such infrastructure to be accepted as well, as long as they remain there.

That's a more reasonable approach, and increasingly common. It also highlights a hidden motivation: the "big three" (AWS, GCP, Azure) are usually deemed safe. It's not because they are "provably safer"; all these CISOs who manage these wasteful processes that ensure security of their vendors appear perfectly happy with merely downloading the audit reports for the cloud vendors, no RFP required. The simple reason is that, by being so big, these three tend to host amongst them the vast majority of SaaS vendors. Even so, some CISOs remain firmly opposed, feeling that this healthy business practice places a *personal* risk of pre-acceptance on their shoulders.

This problem becomes more acute when it comes to data, and in particular when we add yet another layer of abstraction—the platform-as-a-service (PaaS) provider. These cloud-based service providers handle customer data as *incidental* to their primary service, which is to provide a virtual *platform*. Customer data indeed transitions the PaaS virtual systems, but PaaS personnel do not interact with it, and their platform does not make decisions based on any (human) knowledge of the data; rather, it acts on the data algorithmically as instructed by the customers.

The easiest conceptual example of that is a data proxy, a system which provides hookups for any other system in order to facilitate data migrations from one external system to another. Based in the cloud, this is a pure PaaS play: the platform has all the capabilities required to handle data transformations, but the platform vendor and, in particular, their personnel are "unaware" of how the customers utilize the platform to do so. This is like another cloud layer, seeing as clouds are also platforms. If you think of the cloud as a virtual hard drive and CPU, then the PaaS is a virtual application *server* (and a SaaS is a virtual *application*).

How will a PaaS vendor address their customer's security concerns? They do not interact with the data directly, but rather as a side effect, and even then, have no real concept of the nature of the data that traverses the system boundaries. Heck, the best ones will insist on not implementing any direct data control that implies knowledge of the underlying data, if for nothing else than for liability and self-preservation purposes. Put another way, a security-minded PaaS vendor *doesn't know* what data the customers push through their platform, and *doesn't care* about it, either, because they rightly consider it to be none of their business (what I like to call the "we don't know, we don't care" principle).

It is, in fact, the same exact principle that the cloud provider itself (Amazon, Google, Microsoft, et al.) follows. We give you a sandbox, but what you do with it is up to you.

It's just one more level of abstraction.

The data transformations themselves also take place on somebody else's systems, that is, the cloud company. Faced with questions about data protection, it can become difficult, even impossible, to answer them in a satisfactory way, without some level of absurdity. For example, how does this hypothetical PaaS vendor answer the question "do you protect sensitive data at rest?" Why is this such a challenging question? Because the vendor is fundamentally unaware of any distinction within customer data, what is sensitive and not sensitive. Further, to add a capability to do so will, by necessity—since it would involve the vendor becoming aware of what customer data is sensitive in order to make a determination of security controls—ultimately *lower the overall security posture of the platform for the enterprise customer*. I'll mention the most obvious reason: it violates the basic yet important principle of "need to know."

The PaaS vendor thus must adopt a viewpoint, and will often find that an actual attempt to be honest and discuss the very nature of a public-cloud-based PaaS only leads to legal and sales barriers, even when the truth is that they just treat all data the same way, and (hopefully) give customers additional security controls (such as encryption key management) to apply to their data in any manner the customer deems appropriate.

It is in both the vendor and the customer's best interests that the vendor provides controls and the customer applies them as necessary. But the security questionnaire will practically never account for this subtlety, and the enterprise legal department even less so.

This expanded and highly abstracted sphere of data control is probably the biggest overall security issue in the modern world of cloud. These issues are rarely resolved in contract, at least not without a very delicate and informed touch, and that requires a significant amount of knowledge on the side of the enterprise counsel and their security chief, as well as the vendor's security leader, who must be able, knowledgeable, and experienced enough to support legal negotiations to a successful resolution that will not introduce hidden risk and liability down the road.

With that said, there are some useful open-ended questions that should be asked by any enterprise of every cloud vendor that they are considering. Note that this is intentionally short and open-ended, since the goal here is to get an insight into the security mindset of the vendor, rather than dictate by implication a list of expected security controls.

SHORT ESSAY

BASIC QUESTIONS TO ASK YOUR CLOUD SAAS/ PAAS VENDOR

1 Do you use (insert list of internally pre-approved cloud providers here) as your cloud provider?
   a If not, which cloud provider do you use?
   b If you use more than one cloud provider, name all of them and their function.

2 During your initial selection and up to this point in time, what measures have you taken to check your cloud provider's security and compliance posture?

    a Do you validate your cloud provider's security and compliance posture on an ongoing basis? How? Please provide evidence of the most recent review.

3 Do you have a formal internal information security program?

    a If yes, does it include:

        i Security policies? (please list them)

        ii Business Continuity Plan (BCP)?

            A If yes, what is the frequency of testing, and when was it last tested?

            B If not, do you plan to develop one? When will it be complete?

        iii Disaster Recovery Plan (DRP)?

            A If yes, what is the frequency of testing, and when was it last tested?

            B If not, do you plan to develop one? When will it be complete?

        iv Incident Response Plan (IRP)?

            A If yes, has it been triggered in the last 12 months? Please share any information you can relate to the triggering event and its resolution.

        v Software Development Life Cycle (SDLC)?

            A If yes, what measures does it have to explicitly address information security?

    b Do you have a formal security compliance program? If so, please name the standards you comply with, and include all current internal and external validation of such compliance.

4 Do you have a formally assigned individual or group accountable to information security in your

organization, such as a CISO or ISC? How is it organized internally?

5   Do you perform security testing in any portion of your environment?

    a   If so, please list the types of testing (e.g., penetration testing, vulnerability scanning, code reviews, etc.), their scope, and frequency.

    b   What was the most recent date when each type of test took place? Did you successfully remediate the findings from the tests?

    c   Does your testing process include post-remediation validation? If not, please name the types of tests that do not.

6   What sensitive data or PII will you handle (store, process, or transmit) on behalf of our company?

    a   How long will our sensitive data be stored in your environment? Can we modify this period?

    b   If sensitive data is stored, please describe how it is protected from unauthorized access and leaks.

7   What type of access is necessary for this engagement (e.g., VPN to our data center, remote login)?

    a   Which access control measures do you support?

    b   Can we integrate any form of SSO or federated logins into your environment? If so, which ones?

8   Is your environment fully or partially multi-tenant?

    a   If yes, please describe how our company's data is segregated from other customers.

    b   What security event logs will be available to us, and in what form?

9   If a security incident occurs which potentially impacts our company, how quickly will we be notified? What would trigger such notification?

    a   Do you maintain forensic audit trails? Which ones? Will we have access to them?

It is worth reiterating that the goal here is not to cover every possible control, or indeed to define an acceptable level of controls. The nature of the answers to these open-ended questions will tend to indicate the level of security thinking at the vendor. For example, the SDLC question is intentionally vague, and the answers will be indicative. Would the vendor list data retention controls? How about third-party OSS library license crosschecks? The answer to question 6 about handling sensitive data will be indicative; a response along the lines of "we don't know, it's up to you" is probably a good one! (the "we don't know/care" principle in play).

Critically, this is it! Don't also send them the big questionnaire, which is pointless anyway.

With so much embedded risk, an experienced security leader becomes essential. An ability to understand the differences between different kinds of software and service providers, different operational and strategic business drivers, and legal and liability challenges inherent in such engagements will give them a unique risk management perspective and allow them to inform the business initiative process in a way that can be invaluable in the long term.

Properly understood in this role as a technology and data risk manager, the CISO can contribute in many ways:

- *They can steer the company away from potentially costly R&D decisions.* In one example, a lead developer in a large multinational requested our advice with respect to a new, major m-commerce feature release, which would involve a significant intake of behavioral PII into the general e-commerce platform. Aware of upcoming privacy regulations in the EU, one of our recommendations was to implement a way to allow any consumer to request the removal of all their PII from the company's systems—we called it the "big red button" library—as a way to address the soon-to-be regulated "right to be forgotten." This library could be called with an identifier, and automatically remove all PII related to that identifier. The developer was delighted, since at that stage in the design process, implementing such a feature would be trivial. Alas—and as an unfortunate demonstration of the potential internal conflict between security and the business—2 weeks later we were informed that Legal instructed the development team to not implement such a feature, and worse, to make it virtually impossible to remove any consumer's PII from the company's systems *without a massive manual undertaking*. Their argument was that based on U.S. law, this would allow the company to avoid ever having to remove such data because it would be prohibitively costly to the business. That decision was ultimately never tested because the platform folded before it could face the EU regulator over GDPR, but I imagine it could have been fairly interesting if it had.

- *They can reduce structural technology business risk while removing growth obstacles*, for example, by independent review and pre-acceptance of popular cloud platforms, maybe with a defined set of embedded controls and configurations (also known as "swim lanes").

- *They can help draft legal language that makes sense in abstracted contexts*. This is especially true in the cloud provider space, where boundaries of liability and responsibility can get pretty murky. One adjunct to this is for the security leader to be very customer-friendly, and become an integral part of the sales process, providing education and reassurance, often in direct conversation with their counterpart on the side of the prospective enterprise customer.

- *They can participate in M&A processes to try and uncover hidden or unexpected deal blockers*. I was once invited to participate in due-diligence meetings related to a multi-billion-dollar merger. I was introduced as the CIO's advisor, and was expected to listen, and possibly note anything that the team may have otherwise missed. In fact, the CIO's request was phrased thusly: "you always have good questions. Maybe you'll have one for us here, too." Well, long story short, I did at some point have a question, about the possibility of risk and regulatory costs related to the combining of the two companies' rather different cultures and practices around data use, and in particular, the vast troves of consumer-sensitive data they were both managing. I was informed later that this issue became central for a short time and the regulators did ultimately get involved, but thankfully, the team on "our side" was aware of the challenge in advance and was prepared to address it, which helped smooth the transaction process.

• *They can assist through the power of negative inference thinking.*

Alright, I fully admit that the latter point is a teaser.

So what is this "power of negative thinking" concept?

Let's go back to business school for a minute. Having gone through a fairly respectable MBA program back in Israel before I came to the United States, I even managed to retain a couple of things. One of them was the strong bias toward action–reaction decision chains.

What do I mean by that? Well, generally speaking, business culture (at least in the west) seems to be focused on actions and reactions. Put another way, the most common question one gets asked is "what do we do now?" (action), often followed by "how do we answer this development?" (reaction). This action bias often leads companies to do great things, but just as often, it can lead them into chasing ghosts, and more importantly, miss massive market trends building right under their noses.

Why is that? Because if the new trend represents a significant enough shift from the existing model, it may not register on the market analysis needles until it's too late. There will be little, if anything, to which to respond. This is how large companies grow complacent and are then upstaged by youthful startups.

It's merely the entire foundation for the existence of Silicon Valley.

But consider the CISO, and especially their training. In particular, good CISOs are uniquely qualified to handle these sorts of "negative information" trends. Why? Because they are trained to spot trends both when there is an abundance of data, and also when there is a notable *lack of* abnormal activity. For a CISO, either one of these scenarios is suspicious. The latter may indicate a particularly stealthy compromise attempt (using the electronic version of "move along, nothing to see here" approach), one that normalizes patterns so as to be the least likely to be detected. This particular issue is going to become much bigger in the near future, as behavior-based systems will begin confronting behavior-based attacks that try to fool them into accepting bad behavior as good, but that is a topic for another book (2nd edition note: this suggestion has also, thus far, played out as predicted). Incidentally, that's why good hackers can be valuable as part of a computer defense strategy; they can "sniff out" these kinds of patterns instinctively; bug bounty programs work.

Now imagine being able to shape one's experience in this sort of detection into a business tool. Give your good CISO the training and foundation to translate this ability into the business realm, name them as a board advisor, and then let them provide input into the quarterly board meetings. Just let them tell you what they see.

Who knows? They may see something nobody else does, precisely because it is invisible.

Even if not, at the very least you will have discovered a potential source of new business leaders that can help your company deal with an unexpected, rapid shift in your market or the economy at large. And they will be delighted to have some sort of career path beyond being CISO.

2.2

INCIDENTS, SCHMINCIDENTS

One topic comes up regularly these days: security incidents and breaches. Yes, the ghosts that keep us up at night. The reason we keep insisting that the CISO's job is to "protect the company."

Hackers.

Ransomware.

You know, the scary stuff.

That you can buy a lot of books on how to set up a cyber infrastructure that will help prevent such an event from occurring, even if you follow all of their advice, should do nothing to alleviate your concerns.

Let me take this a step further: I have yet to meet a single person in security or otherwise that, after implementing all the best cyber practices and spending even many millions on software tools, truly sleeps well at night in the comfort of knowing that they are "secure."

That they have prevented a breach from ever occurring.

Not one. And in truth, most practitioners don't have unlimited resources or the ability to enforce best practices uniformly across the organization.

Because, you know, businesses do business.

Not cyber.

Even security vendors are there to sell product.

A very basic reality check exposes the fallacy of cyber "defense" as some sort of goal: just read the news headlines and see the ever-growing list of truly impressive brand names who have been publicly hacked. Now consider the ones not made public. It's just the tip of the iceberg. I know it, and you know it.

Everyone knows it.

Since I see part of my job in this text to calm people down, I wish to poke at this, because if we can get through this intact, the rest is easy.

DOI: 10.1201/9781003302759-5

Let's start with a simple question: what is, actually, a security incident?

Ah.

It used to be that a *security incident* was a catchall phrase that described practically everything going bad, from a single user's laptop catching a virus to a massive breach of PII. Unfortunately, with time, the term has become loaded. This is due to its overuse in contractual language, where enterprise brands regularly attempt to overreach into their vendors' security programs, as well as in the legal and regulatory arena, where lawmakers have written laws requiring public notification of these events while misusing the term.

As a result, the word "incident" is no longer safe to use. It has too much baggage. It's the derogatory term du-jour of the security world. Would you have to call the newspapers every time one of your employees' computers has a virus? That would be preposterous.

Even if there are some people who really want it to happen. One obvious constituency are class-action lawyers, a.k.a. ambulance chasers.

But what, then, should qualify as an incident?

And, perhaps even more importantly, what differentiates an incident from a breach?

Let me start with a story to illustrate how even highly respected security leaders often go astray here.

I was serving in the role of transitional CISO for an extremely high-growth company, one of those tech firms that was breaking out big. This is a role I play occasionally, as the old guard finds that what they used to love in a small startup is rapidly changing, and senior leadership decides it's time to level up. It usually only lasts for a few months, but it's a high-impact engagement, because I am able to set a course and help the organization hire the right kind of full-time candidate.

I cherish these opportunities.

In this case, I failed.

Well, I may be a bit harsh with myself here. What happened was that they ended up with two very qualified and likeable candidates and asked me which of them should be hired. My advice was to hire the one that was a bit less polished but more attuned to the needs of a hypergrowth company like theirs. They opted to go instead with the very polished fella with the large company experience. It seemed like this would run a fairly high risk of rapid alienation between the incoming CISO and the rest of the senior staff, a classic example of setting the new guy up to fail.

While there is some virtue in hiring forward, there is also a pretty hard limit on how far forward you can hire.

In another unusual turn of events, they almost immediately wrapped up our engagement. Typically this isn't the case; most companies feel that it's worth having me as an advisor, and my team as backup, once we have engaged. This new CISO wanted absolutely nothing to do with me or my team, because they came from big companies with big in-house teams. They didn't need us, and he certainly didn't want me "interfering" with his work.

They wanted to build their own team.

I came to learn of this less than a year later, when the founder called me and opened the conversation by saying, with a laugh, that "you told us so." They were going to let the guy go because he had burned himself within the company. And the way he did it is a powerful illustration of many of the principles we discuss in this book, and ties directly to the issue of security incidents.

So what did he do?

In an effort to "increase visibility" for security within the organization, he chose to lean heavily on the incident response process (IRP). As an aside, why you would want to reinforce the idea that security is scary, by making sure that the primary mode of communications between you and the rest of senior leadership is around the very things that scare them, is quite beyond me. I see it happen a lot, and I still don't get it.

Anyway.

I knew what their previous IRP looked like—it was reasonable for a company their size, with tickets being managed in the ticketing system, and several tags used to identify different types of security events (like viruses or phishing or what have you). It wasn't flashy, but it worked, and since there wasn't that much going on incident-wise, it served its purpose sufficiently well.

But it wasn't very *visible*.

So our new guy created a much more significant IRP, including two major changes: the first was reclassifying many things that previously were not considered "incidents" (I had previously cautioned folks about the word and its emotional baggage) into incidents. The second was making sure that *everybody* in senior staff knew about them.

Like, all of them.

All the time.

This clearly came from good intentions; if we think of our role as security leaders in terms of "protecting the company," then letting others know *how* we are doing it seems sensible, especially if we want to encourage them to think of our protective duty as important.

You could have profitably predicted the outcome with odds of 10-1 against.

After a few months, the CEO grew irate and demanded that the fella explain why, since he was brought on board, the company began having all these security incidents.

"Hold on a moment," I hear you say. The incidents were there all along. All the guy did was point them out.

Precisely.

Pointing them out was the first error.

Then, when challenged, he doubled down and explained the very obvious thing about the incidents always being there. And with that, he started the final countdown for his inevitable exit. Because the CEO was right; the only reason the company started having all these incidents was because the CISO *chose to call them incidents.*

It's not like the number or velocity of incidents increased.

The change wasn't on the ground.

It was in communications about the incidents.

How do I know?

Because after I was brought in again to again help them transition between CISOs, I discovered that all these new incidents were, in reality, the very same things they used to have—primarily, issues with their product code that led to potential or actual vulnerabilities.

Bugs.

Their engineers found most of them, and their clients found a few as well (hey, it happens everywhere).

A couple of them even resulted in uncomfortable moments where privacy counsel had to make a determination as to whether they required limited notification, but ultimately decided they didn't.

Critically, they happened *at the same rate they used to happen before the CISO came onboard.*

This strategy could have worked, with a lot of preparation and a deft personal touch to ensure that this extra visibility was appreciated. And that was the second, critical error: the assumption that anybody, by default, cared to hear about this stuff.

Nobody wants to hear it, people.

Stop freaking out your peers and bosses!

So the guy was toast.

His experience, though, is helpful to us in terms of understanding what makes for an incident nowadays.

Generally speaking, a *security incident* should at this point in the evolution of the practical discipline be thought of as an *actual* compromise of a mission-critical system. And the word "compromise" in this instance means involving *external* parties. If one of our employees on payroll screws up a security configuration, that simply does not qualify.

Sorry.

Even if it manifests a vulnerability (more on that in a second).

A *breach* is where you actually lose customer data to external parties who are not already within your ecosystem. So, a configuration error that led to, say, one customer's data ending up in the bucket of another for a limited amount of time is an *incident*, not a *breach*.

For everything else, find some other terminology you like ("events" works nicely here). A configuration error leading to some customer data ending up in a development bucket? An event, although you may have to tell that customer it happened. Importantly, that determination is up to counsel, not the security leader, since the necessity of such action is a contractual issue, not a security operations one.

Vulnerabilities are another touchy topic. Vulnerabilities are *potential* incidents, but they are not, in and of themselves, anything beyond that. The existence of vulnerabilities does not ever require notification, nor is it an incident of any kind. Hope you find them before they manifest into an incident, fix them as best you can . . . and move on.

No need to get into a tizzy about it.

Remember the CISO from the previous chapter who left his private company in a huff? At one point, I asked him politely which regulators needed to be notified about the company's horrible vulnerability management practices, and in what fashion. I never got an answer.

Companies can and do choose to use outdated software, and part of the job of security leaders is to help engineers get over that hump. But usually when this happens, there is a good, product reason for it, just like it was in this case, and so change is difficult. Time for a hard truth: Living with risk—not just eliminating it—is part of a CISO's job!

For what it's worth, as of now anyway, nothing bad ever came of that whole fiasco. Not a breach, not an incident, not even an event, and the company hasn't blown up.

Clearly, the message to security leaders here is "dial it down a notch." See beyond the edge of your nose. You want people to care about what you do; that's understandable. We all want that. Just remember that your employer's goals are business ones.

Not cyber ones.

If you can adjust in this one way, you will do yourself (and everyone around you) a world of good.

3

LET IT RAIN

The sales VP is nervous.

This is potentially a very large client, and an international one at that. The quarter is going to close soon, and the security RFP he just got from his regional rep seems endless and also a little different than the rest.

When he forwards it to me, he also calls and tells me that this deal is particularly critical; the company will be going for another round of funding soon, and international expansion is a specific business metric the investors are going to examine. He tells me emphatically he knows he's in good hands (the guy is good at his job).

When I send him the responses a couple of days later in preparation for the call with their security team, he calls me back almost immediately. "What do you mean, you won't answer this question?" he demands, with a tone of disbelief clearly evident. I ask him what he's referring to. "It says so right here . . . you wrote that we will not answer this question prior to the phone conference."

I know the question to which he is referring. It was a funny one. It said, "On a scale of one to ten, please rate your company's overall security posture." It's a strange one, and I smell a trap.

He goes on, "Why not just answer it? I know we are doing great, just put a nine or a ten in there."

I tell him he's going to have to trust me on this one. Thankfully, we have a solid relationship, and he says, "I will, but don't blow this. We really need this deal to close this quarter."

The call is the next morning. We go through the motions. We get to the question. They ask me why I refused to answer it.

DOI: 10.1201/9781003302759-6

I say, simply, that I would not consider myself a good security leader if I ever felt that my company's security posture is perfect or near perfect, and so the most I would ever be willing to rate it at is a seven or eight. I go on to suggest that if I put that in the RFP response, the sales VP would find a way to climb through the email system and eat me alive, winter jacket and all.

Right as I finish saying that, I get a Slack message from our guy demanding: where the hell are you going with this?!

I add that I had a feeling that this question is designed to find out more about *how* we respond rather than *what* we say.

After everyone laughs at that, they respond.

"Well done," their CISO says. "It's rare that we encounter such a level of maturity at a service provider." He confirms that my take on the question is exactly right. We wrap things up quickly and the deal ultimately closes on time.

After the call, the sales VP calls me to thank me and promise me yet another drink. And then he says this: "you have balls. I like that. And somehow you always make it work with the customers. I like that even better."

It's a wonderful compliment, and a much better thank you than anything else he could have offered.

To be honest, I don't drink much, anyway.

Do you work for a security products or services vendor?

If so, then the idea that security sells is far from being foreign to you.

The state of the security industry is such that it is, at present, very highly fragmented. It sometimes seems that new security vendors are popping up daily, each with a highly specialized take on a narrow niche, which, if extrapolated fantastically (yet still fairly logically), affects *everyone* and *everything* on a massive scale.

Or maybe you work at a retail bank, which makes your employer both a (1) place where consumer trust is hard to win and paramount to doing business; and (2) highly appetizing target for technology enabled fraud. You even know what phishing means (the various techniques used in attempting to lure unsuspecting end-users into disclosing their private information, such as access credentials to their online banking portal, with the goal of cleaning it out shortly thereafter).

Work in e-commerce, maybe? Is it important to make consumers trust your site? It's certainly not a given, and even a 1% improvement in conversion rates (or similar reduction in fraud) can mean a lot of revenue for a larger brand. The numbers are usually bigger, sometimes a lot bigger.

In fact, I'd argue that most industries are coming round to the understanding that lack of proper security positioning and messaging may be a sales blocker. This is particularly apparent in (again) the cloud space, where SaaS/PaaS vendors have to regularly satisfy detailed security requirements from their enterprise customers.

Yet, to be blunt, almost everyone seems to be flailing about with no clear direction, reinventing the wheel over and over again.

Why should we do this?

In enterprises, security questionnaires aimed at vetting vendors rapidly devolve into an exercise in shifting legal liability and minimizing liability exposure. This is good as far as it goes, but while it is an impressive exercise in merging information security and contract law, it also rapidly escalates into a realm that is far removed from practical security considerations. These questionnaires get taken over by legal considerations (and their language becomes legalistic) as part of a misguided attempt to transform them into contractual elements. They become overly complicated and hold up contracts that would otherwise be straightforward. This results in a hidden but cumulatively significant drag on sales, productivity, and growth.

Often, smaller service providers find themselves in a position of agreeing to things they do not necessarily understand, and definitely cannot represent, simply out of desperation. To survive, they have to find a way to get through a process that can seem impossible to navigate.

The classic business cycle plays its traditional role here. Once the vendor gets that first big brand-name (logo) client, they can use them to get others, and eventually drive the terms and conditions into a more comfortable position. Note, however, that this evolution has nothing to do with security controls, even though security is ostensibly under discussion. I highly doubt that many of these vendors have ever gone back to their earlier customers to update their original security answers. A few very large enterprises do ask for such updates, but that still doesn't change the fundamental truth: the answers are only provided on a best effort, point-in-time basis.

It's another version of "fake it till you make it."

Worse, the business managers nominally doing the vetting on the customer side are usually ill-informed as well. Security is not their realm, but the security department has proven itself to be aloof and unresponsive to their needs. Their relationship with their internal security folks has become a frustrating experience in checkboxing, similar to many compliance initiatives. Instead of actually helping identify and mitigate risk, the focus becomes an exercise in shifting liability—a useful one, no doubt, from the perspective of corporate lawyers, but not one that really serves its stated security purpose.

You may be saying to yourself right now, "I get it, Barak, but how else would we find out if our vendor is legit? How do we cover our asses?" In response, let me ask you this. When was the last time you heard of a security manager actually stopping a business manager from going through a transaction that the latter really truly needed to execute to support mission-critical business operations? I don't mean during the negotiations. I mean honest-to-goodness *this shalt not happen because I don't trust the vendor's security posture* type of hard stop. If you've ever been part of the vetting process, the dirty little secret is that it seems as if, as the pressure builds, someone (usually the vendor) eventually relents to agreeing to something that they shouldn't, a checkbox gets checked, a form is completed, and the deal gets signed. And you know who is usually not involved in these last-minute exchanges?

You guessed it. The buyer's security department, other than getting the magically completed security due diligence form, nicely packaged with the expected reassurances from the business manager.

Everybody is happy, and business soldiers on.

The vendor's security posture remains identical, of course.

Let me ask you this: what's the point?

IT'S A VERY, VERY LARGE DEAL

It involves one of the biggest telecomm companies. Our company (for whom I am the CISO) has been really wanting to break into the space, and rightly so. It's a huge opportunity for growth.

The lawyer managing the contract reaches out to me. She tells me that she doesn't think we can do it without promising things she already knows we shouldn't promise, like the right to audit facilities to which we don't even have access.

There is, of course, no way the deal is not happening because of security. Our enterprise sales folks are an understanding bunch, but not that understanding.

The way she puts it to me, it sounds like a pretty solid argument. This customer has to deal with all sorts of rules and regulations, and there is no question of their modifying their required terms, especially not for a deal with a fairly young company like ours.

She doesn't know what to do, but sends the contract to me anyway.

I read through the security addendum, a 50+ page monster that, when you break it down to component requirements, doesn't say anything we are not already doing. In fact, I am somewhat surprised to find that, nestled between all the astoundingly wasteful amount of legalese, is a somewhat intelligently crafted set of security control criteria. That is definitely not par for the course.

But there are some things we simply cannot do without breaking our model. Sure, we could promise that we do them—it is, after all, the time-honored method of dealing with this sort of thing—but I've worked so hard to train our legal folks to be on the lookout for these tricky security-related clauses that I come up against my own strong internal resistance to taking this approach.

Oh, who am I kidding? I hate it. Especially as it doesn't serve any real purpose.

We set up a call with the contract manager at the telecomm.

She explains in a bored tone that, while she completely understands and sympathizes with our position, there is no changing the language of the addendum. Their security department has decided that their rules hold, and so either we sign it and have a deal, or we don't and won't.

"Cathy," I ask her, "I wonder if they would allow a single statement alteration . . ."

"No," she cuts me off. "No alterations."

"I get that," I insist, "But I'm not talking about the addendum language, just the lead-in."

"The lead-in?" she asks, incredulously.

"Yes," I say.

"Go on," she says.

"Well, here is the thing. Clearly we are in a no-win position; we do everything you want us to do, except that in some cases we simply don't exercise control over the related infrastructure, since it resides in the cloud. So we would effectively be breaking the contract by signing it, which is something neither of us wants. Right?"

"Right," she says.

"So how about instead of committing to things both you and I know we can't commit to, why don't we add a single statement at the end of the lead-in that explicitly exempts us from managing the technical provisions of the addendum we have no control over, while maintaining our liability in representing that they are in place, since we know that our cloud provider has them? We are not changing any of the control requirements this way."

A few seconds pass as she considers.

"I hadn't thought of that," she finally responds, "Let me get back to you."

A couple of days later our lawyer gets back to me. "They took it!" she gushes and thanks me profusely. "I'm so going to use this in the future!"

Enterprises often also miss opportunities to capitalize on security as a way to build their brand. If you look at security as something the IT department does—essentially a backoffice component of the organization—then it is no surprise that you would never consider how they could be helpful to the launch of a new product.

Yet often security input can indeed be quite helpful. In an age where consumer loyalty is increasingly harder to attain and maintain, especially for larger brands, every edge matters. Some organizations come to understand this almost by way of survival; retail banks will generally at least make a faint attempt toward reassuring their customers that their information (and money!) is safe. But in a world where smart products are becoming the norm, so many established product makers seem to miss an obvious opportunity to build trust.

"Our connected fridge will never spy on you, because it is a secure connected fridge" may sound a bit ridiculous, but does tap into the public consciousness.

Still, I am not a marketer, so let's go to the next step.

There are opportunities to both sell security and gain trust at the same time. Let me suggest a hypothetical scenario from the world of social networking.

Or the way my daughter would put it, let's talk about Facebook, duh.

Why shouldn't Facebook offer a paid privacy option?

After all, the value of the company is derived from the value of its network, which in turn is derived from the value of its consumer profiles and behaviors as it pertains to advertising and ancillary services. There is an actual dollar amount that Facebook assigns internally to its users, which conveniently (at least if you read through the boring stuff) happens to be part of its financial disclosures as a public company.

So why not offer a privacy-conscious user the option to "redeem their value" for a year in return for a "Privacy Shield"? In this hypothetical scenario, Facebook will, say, suppress all tracking and advertising for that user for the period of subscription, in return for the subscription fee. In theory, this approach could gain in several ways. First, consumers will be much better informed about how much value they are actually getting in "free" services. Second, those who are truly privacy conscious would have a way to remain within and still utilize the network. And third, consumer trust in Facebook would increase overall, because the company would appear to be so much more transparent.

Of course, this is intentionally an overly simplistic example, and I am ignoring a bunch of related issues, but it does serve to illustrate the point: security can at least propose ways to help the brand while staying focused on security's primary mission, which is to reduce overall risk.

When selling to businesses (instead of consumers), there is normally a lot more room to insert security messaging and shape product offerings in a way that would build stickiness. Yet, outside of security product vendors, this almost always seems like an afterthought. Often the "security posture" question—how strong the security program of the vendor might be—only gets addressed after a customer asks about it, and the first-time customers ask these questions is usually when the vendor first attempts to sign a deal with a large enterprise account. That is, incidentally, exactly when the sales pressure and stakes are at their highest.

I would submit that, outside of everything we have discussed thus far, this particular juncture may not be the ideal time for the CISO and the sales executive to seriously engage with each other for the first time.

Yet herein lies a significant opportunity, because those enterprise customers are used to getting a "deer in the headlights" kind of response. A vendor that actually comes back with a competent, well-articulated answer to these questions can often get through the acquisition process more quickly and smoothly, engendering loyalty with the acquiring business manager that reached out to them in the first place. While they would never admit it, they are secretly grateful to have avoided the typical tortured back-and-forth with their own internal security department.

Which is precisely where a competent, externally facing, sales-and-customer-friendly CISO can really shine and deliver the kind of value that matters to the business.

The boardroom is quieting down after the initial chitchat, waiting for the CEO to speak. He goes through the various items one expects to hear in such meetings—financial goals, market positioning, and so on, and gets to the topic of sales and projections. The head of sales confirms that the company is on track to hit its goals.

The CEO turns to me and asks about the company's security program. I am secretly delighted to have gotten to the point where the CEO cares about this issue enough that I am there to make a short presentation. I do so quickly, indicating at the end that it is my belief that we have achieved the CEO's most important objective, which is to remove security as a sales barrier. The company's services are not directly related to security, but its enterprise customers do use them to handle their sensitive data, so security always comes up in the acquisition process.

The CEO turns to the head of sales and asks him directly, "Is this true?" He's a solid guy who likes to be direct about things, rather than pussyfoot around them.

The head of sales looks at me, smiles and turns to the CEO.

"Yes," he says. "In fact, not only is it no longer an obstacle, now it's an advantage. When I talk to prospects, they tell me that they know we are leaders in our security, and it makes it easier for them to work with us."

The CEO says, "That's great! I'm glad to hear that." Then he proceeds to ask, "Did you notice an interruption or slowdown to business activity or the ability to operate because of security?" The response is a clear affirmation that, indeed, no such interruption has taken place.

Satisfied, he moves on to the next topic.

One of the greatest allies that a CISO can have in their (for-profit) organization is the head of sales. If the former can help the latter remove sales barriers, and maybe even increase their sales at the margins, then they will become far more valuable to the organization at large. And yet, I find that many security leaders fail to engage with sales except when absolutely required to do so, often showing disdain for sales people and the sales organization in the process. This is not hugely surprising, considering that so many security people are engineers on steroids, and technical folks have always had a rocky relationship with sales.

I mean, come on. Surely you have read a Dilbert cartoon at least once.

But as I hope is becoming clear by now, it is a massive, failed opportunity. Security can enable sales to

- *Remove sales barriers*: By anticipating and addressing customer concerns around security and privacy in advance, assisting sales and marketing in creating the proper messaging and collateral, and even training sales people in how to handle the basic security conversation, security can make a positive contribution to the sales process. Creating "packets of collateral" that include current audit letters, marketing one-pagers discussing security, and similar items can help a sales person immensely in navigating the initial round of questions from customers, and enabling them to build the trust that is so essential to closing the deal. Developing a program to answer RFPs from customers can be essential to closing big deals. Sales people pretty much always appreciate sales tools, and in that, I mean things like basic insights and language that can help them address tricky questions upfront and close deals faster, without having to involve the technical people. This means that a small investment of time in developing good answers to anticipated security questions and popularizing them with sales is an excellent investment in internal relationship building, and shows an almost immediate return for the company. I often find myself reminding colleagues that the sales department brings in the money that pays their hefty salaries. Sadly, I get scoffed at just as regularly.

- *Increase stickiness*: Customer loyalty is hard to come by, and security represents an area where a positive perception can create a competitive advantage. A good security program and relevant messaging can go beyond enabling the sale. For the smart vendor, it can also create a sales barrier for the competition down the road. A customer that feels safe in your hands is a customer that will be reluctant to go somewhere else.

- *Create upsell opportunities*: Because security represents such an important and often not very well understood intersection of business and technology, security leaders are in a position that can directly contribute to the bottom line. Many offerings—especially in hosted or cloud service environments—lend themselves naturally to security messaging and premium features. Yet often these opportunities go unnoticed.

Say what?

Let's explore that last one a little bit more.

Conceptually, what I mean is that the CISO should consider whether any technology acquisition or portions of the security program can be expanded in such a way as to support the company's business.

There are some obvious forms of upsell opportunities around security, such as additional product features offered as premium add-ons (perhaps to nudge customers from a free to a paid product tier). Single-sign-on (SSO) and 2-factor/2-channel integration is a trivial example. SSO support should be implemented, both internally (for the company's use) and externally (for the customers' use), using the same technology.

A vendor can identify such opportunities in conjunction with adding security controls to their own environment. This is where security and Go-to-Market interaction is critical; the security team would need to identify the opportunity, and actually remember to engage with sales to see whether it might also be a good fit for customers.

That will never happen if the CISO doesn't envision their job in the context of sales enablement, or the VP of sales doesn't even remember the CISO's name, except when he or she absolutely has to talk to them.

In another area where such collaboration is ripe with opportunity, many software vendors these days operate using a freemium model— basic service is free, but for premium features, one must pay a subscription fee. In many cases, these premium features are what makes the product truly desirable to more than the casual end-user. Here are some examples of security controls that can easily be converted into premium add-ons (or bundled into an "enterprise" version) that would fit neatly into most cloud-based services models:

- *Customizable data retention controls*: Providing customers with the ability to trigger automated data removals based on data aging, or maybe preserve data for certain predetermined periods of time to satisfy their own regulatory requirements.
- *Logging and monitoring*: Assuming the security program at the vendor is mature enough that security events are already being centralized, correlated, and alerted, it may be a simple matter to create an API for customers interested in (and willing to

pay for) them to directly obtain a contextual feed of such logs. Incidentally, this control can also reduce discovery costs when something bad does happen and the lawyers get involved.

- *Enhanced access control*: Multifactor authentication is a big crowd-pleaser these days, but we can go beyond that, as we explore in another sample scenario below.
- *Enhanced encryption key management*: The options abound here. Why not allow customers to choose algorithms and ciphers, manage and rotate their own keys? Or even better, incorporate and offer some sort of split-key mechanism (e.g., homomorphic encryption)?

Note that all of these are controls that a security department would naturally be interested in as part of their primary role in the company. All it takes is asking the question when evaluating new products and vendors: "can our business benefit from incorporating this into our own offerings?"

The value multiplier for the sales-minded CISO arises because the security field is undergoing rapid transformation. The security department will often be exploring bleeding-edge technologies before any other department in the company, if only because attack vectors evolve so rapidly. A security leader with this mindset and an established relationship with sales will be able to correlate new tool acquisitions with the company's Go-to-Market strategy and suggest opportunities to expand the utilization of such tools as part of product or service offerings. For example, let's consider the case of cloud access management. The IT department at the vendor, working with the security department, is considering implementation of a cloud access broker solution to manage access to its various backoffice cloud-based applications, such as in human resources, CRM (Saleforce), and collaboration (yo, Slack).

In this example, the CISO may ask the company's sales team: "would our customers benefit from being able to track, monitor, and report on their users' access to our cloud product?" The answer to that would almost certainly be yes, but the goal here is actually to get the sales team thinking and wondering about the expanded opportunity.

The next question might be asked of the head of business development: "would our customers pay extra for being able to detect and respond to any attempted compromise of their user accounts within our product?"

It's important to note here that the kind of compromise mentioned here is the kind that has nothing to do with the vendor's systems. A common way in which customer user accounts get compromised without implicating the SaaS/PaaS vendor is phishing, where the product isn't compromised at all, but a particular user's account might be. This is a big headache for enterprise IT departments, who are the big buyers of SaaS/PaaS products.

The primary objective is, still, to protect the company's use of its own cloud backoffice applications. But it is entirely possible that by considering a different usage of the proposed solutions the company can also benefit from increased sales, customer retention, and satisfaction, as well as position itself as a more trusted entity, increasing stickiness.

And why shouldn't the CISO help their company compete, anyway?

If you are in security, let me ask you this: no matter how good you are, what on earth makes you believe you can (or even deserve to) continue to advance your career when you've never truly engaged with the business side of the company?

With all due respect, and beyond lip service, why should the CEO even *know who you are*?

It is therefore not just because it "helps sales" that this should matter to the security team. It is worth reiterating that an important benefit for security pros is that, by considering whether they can reuse a new technology to support their company's business, inevitably the team will become more aligned with the business, and as a result, *more successful over time*. I would argue dramatically so. At the very least, the CISO will learn how to pitch technology acquisitions up and across the chain more effectively, improving their own communications and business management skills. They will gain trust from their non-technology peers, become more involved in the daily running of the company, a better business partner, and, ultimately, increase their own job satisfaction and career prospects.

You know.

As in not fail.

Especially in today's world, where everything seems to be constantly on "hacker fire," security-conscious customers would often be willing to pay extra for certain security and privacy-oriented features and offerings. I am reminded of one case where we were helping design a set of security controls for one of our clients' cloud offerings. It quickly became obvious that what was desired from a security perspective would also require disabling some features in the product (specifically around access control). In many environments, what would have followed is an internal argument between engineering and sales, increasing mutual dislike and mistrust, and resulting in a likely display of political power in the form of a veto (from either side).

Instead, we brought sales into the conversation and made a suggestion: we would repackage the product with the proposed security controls as a premium offering and offer it as an option to customers at an extra cost. While it is true that some features would be gone, the overall security of the product would be increased, enough so to offset what was lost *for those customers who cared.*

To the astonishment of the head of engineering, sales jumped on this proposal, and in a week or so we already had several big customers lined up to pay extra for the premium offering. A couple of years later, the company's client-base split itself neatly into two groups: one that felt that the extra coin wasn't worth it and preferred to keep the somewhat looser but slightly more feature-rich environment, and another group who thought it very much was worth it to pay more for less features, but significantly higher security. From their perspective, the features they "lost" were in reality a road-block, as they conflicted with their internal security policies.

Neatly enough, within these two groups, it was the largest (enterprise) customers that were willing to pay the premium, which had a larger positive impact on the bottom line than their representation as a percentage of the total number of customers going that way.

Everyone ended up being happy, simply by virtue of implementing a classic technique prominent in the world of auto sales: using trim levels as a tool for customer segmentation.

We later added a section to the company's user conferences, where we discussed the enhanced approach to security as reflected in our premium offering, and that helped build trust in the brand.

Which leads me to my next topic: the intersection of security and marketing.

"So wait . . . our intended default is to save credit cards in our systems?"

I am sitting in a meeting with the security director, a sales manager, and a marketing manager. We called the meeting because it has come to our attention that the company's e-commerce platform was saving all consumer credit card account numbers for future use, without even asking for approval. The security director and I were fairly certain this was an implementation error, but when we asked the engineering team to fix it, they told us that it was by design, in response to a feature request.

Hence the meeting.

The sales and marketing managers tell us, "Yeah. Consumers like that they don't have to re-enter their credit card each time."

"I get that," I say, "but by not even asking them for approval, we are potentially creating a big exposure for ourselves. Do we have any idea of how many consumers actually prefer to keep their cards on file like that?"

The answer is apparently 30%. That seems unusually high to me. After further discussion, we agree to research this a little. Turns out that 30% is the number of consumers that do not turn off the default selection. It's the old "opt-in" versus "opt-out" question all over again, except for the riskier category of credit card account numbers.

We agree to try reversing the default on a trial basis in a portion of the platform. The checkbox would still be there, but the default setting would be for it to be checked off. At least at that point we could record the storage of cards to an active consumer choice, and limit our potential exposure.

A few weeks later, the results come in: after implementation of the reverse default option, the proportion of users actively choosing to store their cards with us plummeted to less than 3%.

Turns out users didn't really want that feature anywhere near as much as we thought.

The preceding story, which resulted in a platform change combined with a much stronger relationship with the marketing department, illustrates a critical point: sometimes, business assumptions must be tested in a way that only security can identify, because it is only security that is in the position to detect the potential risk and exposure inherent in those assumptions. Marketing surely did not have the bailiwick to consider the benefit of reducing the storage of card data by an order of magnitude. It wasn't their job. But I can assure you that simply mandating the change would have resulted in many frayed edges, also colloquially known as "career inhibitors."

In simple terms, security can help a brand, just as the lack of security can destroy a brand. In the age of increasing awareness around issues of privacy, it is no longer just the enterprise buyer who is aware of issues such as data protection—everyone is an expert on this topic these days. Unfortunately, to paraphrase Pope & Bacon, a little knowledge is a dangerous thing.

Yum, bacon.

Sadly, there is so much confusion around issues of data protection and privacy that even the best-intentioned will be led astray. Understanding privacy regulations is one thing, but navigating the world of conflicting rules, cross-jurisdictional issues, and different compliance needs can be a major headache. Just reconciling the EU rules for privacy together with those in the United States, which is also a big driver behind the (now defunct) safe harbor program, is a matter of significant revenue to companies and lawyers specializing in this area.

As one quick example, the EU GDPR says one must allow consumers to erase their data upon request, but financial requirements within EU countries may require one to retain financial information about EU consumers' transactions for up to 10 years. Good luck sorting that one out without expert advice—and considering the potential risk (up to 4% of a company's global revenue in certain cases) and pressure from the top to address it, I would also add, I hope you find the right expert.

That's before we even discuss the *interpretation* of rulings, in both the legal and technical arenas, or even understand the difference between "compliance" (in the context of standards adherence), "compliance" (in the context of validation and audit), and "compliance" (in the context of reporting and registration). We will explore this particularly sneaky communications pitfall, which can result in serious consequences, later. I would go so far as to argue that the most misunderstood word in information security is the word compliance. This can be of high utility to the enterprising CISO who can wield the compliance cudgel over their CFO's objections and gain ever-increasing budgets, but it does little to help that CISO build trust, make allies, and become a bona-fide member of the senior executive team.

Yet herein lies a great opportunity as well. One of the biggest judgment errors that I perceive security leaders in the enterprise make regularly is that of ignoring, or even rejecting, their role in external company communications.

This is not surprising, considering the highly internal (and tactical) focus in which the role is usually cast. In one large Internet darling company where I spoke to the COO about this role, he was quite visibly taken aback that I should equate the "protection of the company" with the "protection and promotion of the brand." He really wanted the security leader to drill down on the technical and operations aspect of security, and the idea that the CISO (who would be the Chief Privacy Officer as well; ahh, those were the days) would be spending time trying to think up ways to drive up consumer trust was anathema to him. From his perspective, it was at best a nice-to-have, certainly not a critical element of the job. Yet this company suffered—and still does—from consumer trust issues directly related to privacy and handling of personal data such that it had *already identified them as a significant growth barrier*.

How much sense does that make?

By actively supporting sales and marketing, by helping remove sales obstacles, increasing stickiness, and identifying upsell opportunities, by coming up with positive messaging and building trust with the company's customer base, a CISO can *help the company grow*. Doing that happens to have a pretty nice side benefit, since it would allow the CISO to gain a larger influence with the real power brokers within their company, and legitimately earn that seat at the table. It can also help open up those missing advancement opportunities; suffice it to say that CISOs do not at present have an obvious path forward.

This latter point is worth repeating: the CISO is a dead-end job.

More about that later.

As someone who plies his trade in this field, that last bit is also something that I find rather disheartening.

3.2

Fear Mongering

Instead of adding more to this chapter myself, I asked Dr. Todd Jacobs (of CodeGnome fame) if there was something he'd like to say with respect to security sales enablement. Todd is a true luminary of the devops community, a highly respected thought leader and Fortune-500 board advisor, and just a great fella all around. More importantly, for the purposes of this book, Todd and I have arrived at similar conclusions over the course of our very different careers. He has a unique and compelling voice, and it is my honor to share his insights with you.

So, without further ado . . . here's Todd.

Enlightened Self-Interest Always Beats Scare Tactics and Fear-Based Solutions

We've talked a bit about how it can be a mistake to talk about security as a technology rather than as a business enabler. A closely related mistake is to use fear, uncertainty, and doubt (collectively known as "FUD") to solicit support for your security programs. While fear is a powerful motivator, the zombie apocalypse that hasn't (yet) come to pass is something your C-suite peers will quickly learn to tune out.

It's very common to use the fear of a security breach to solicit support for a new security product or program. Maybe you need additional funds to buy a new tool to head off an emerging threat, but the tool doesn't fit into your current budget. You're having trouble explaining to the rest of the leadership team why it's necessary to spend another $50,000 a year on licensing, tooling, and labor to solve a possible future problem that hasn't happened yet. Even if it has happened, whether to your company or other companies in your market, the instinctive calculus of business is to focus on the more-tangible problems of today.

DOI: 10.1201/9781003302759-7

A common-but-doomed tactic is to stress the potential financial losses the company might experience due to such an attack. Costs incurred through regulatory fines, operational disruption, and damage to the company's reputation are frequently cited. Headlines highlighting the newest threat are trotted out. And yet, this approach fails more often than not to gain any meaningful traction among other executives. Let's talk about why.

One way to think of cybersecurity is that good security requires thinking about how systems can fail. While it's almost second nature for security professionals to think about the failure modes of any given system, most people discount unrealized future problems that they don't understand, or that seem unlikely or too far in the future to worry about today. Instead, they prioritize immediate needs and near-term objectives, leaving the problems of the future for...well, the future.

I've made the FUD-based pitch myself and understand why it's usually a mistake. I can still remember a conversation with an executive team that had recently been fined nearly $10M for a data breach. That may not sound like all that much these days, after decades of major breaches with penalties and settlements in the hundreds of millions. Still, at that time $10M was a fairly substantial sum of money even for a large corporation.

The security organization had done a full investigation, identified the process issues and control failures that had enabled the breach, and identified solutions to prevent a similar breach from ever happening again. And yet—"Sally," I said earnestly to the CFO, "we need about $2M in new monitoring equipment, additional public key infrastructure to encrypt data at rest, and additional data storage capacity for more detailed logging to be able to prevent this sort of breach in the future."

Sally thought about this. "That's an additional 20% on top of what this breach has already cost us," she pointed out.

"True. But if you amortize the costs over the next few years while reducing the possibility of more fines and penalties if we're breached again . . ." I started to explain. I pulled out charts and graphs showing the limits the new controls would place on the scope of another data breach, the reduction in our annualized loss expectancy, and all the other qualitative and quantitative data I had painstakingly put together.

But Sally was already shaking her head. "No, we can't afford that," she said. "We're already over the IT and security budgets for this year because of the breach. Besides, just because this happened to us once doesn't mean it will happen again anytime soon."

Recognizing that I'd already lost on the cost-efficiency front, I fell back to a previously prepared position. I had come to the meeting armed with data about the number of attempted breaches each year against the company—at least, the ones they were currently equipped to detect—and industry statistics about the frequency and likelihood of similar breaches being successful. To me and the rest of the security team, these details painted a crisp picture of how unprepared we were for another such breach.

Imagine my shock, though, when I realized my data was just pretty pictures and numbers on a page to Sally. These future possibilities didn't feel particularly real or hair-raisingly imminent to her. She was busy thinking in terms of near-term budget shortfalls rather than potential future problems. In fairness to her, this wasn't even an unreasonable position for her to take from a short-term cost/benefit perspective; it just left the security organization without the resources to prevent such a breach from happening again.

Ultimately, the wind-up was that the loss of $10M was perceived as a one-time cost of doing business. Maybe it would happen again or maybe it wouldn't, but from Sally's perspective the tangible cost of remediation and prevention vastly outweighed the potential costs of another breach at some undefined point in the future.

Looking back on it a few decades wiser, I know from more successful experiences that a better approach than FUD would have been to collaborate with the sales and marketing executives. I would have worked with them first, and then let them sell Sally on the need for the additional $2M in funding we needed. That too would have been a "cost of doing business," but one supported by departments seen as revenue generators rather than cost centers.

Naturally, you're now wondering why they would have helped get that funding for us. That's easily explained through enlightened self-interest. Here's how I've learned to address this challenge since that illuminating conversation with Sally.

Rather than relying on the fear of future events or fear-mongering headlines to make a cost-savings argument to the CFO, I've discovered that enlisting the sales and marketing teams as part of a cohesive strategy to provide a stronger security story to our customers is a much easier and more effective approach. Because of the recent breach, sales and marketing were already getting pushback in the marketplace. This was partly because of the negative headlines, but mostly because the same fear and uncertainty that was so unhelpful internally made potential customers feel unsafe.

Customers were asking themselves—and our sales teams, too—some very uncomfortable questions. Why should they trust us with their data? How could we possibly protect their valuable information going forward?

The sales and marketing teams would have loved the chance to tell customers about how much we'd invested since the breach in protecting their valuable data. They would have been over the moon if they'd been empowered to highlight the various ways the company was now committed to protecting customers' information more vigorously than any of their competitors.

Maybe this just sounds like public relations spin to you, but customer confidence is hard to win and easy to lose. Building a solid security strategy around increasing customer confidence is a great way to get to "yes." Rather than preventing a future event, a stronger security story resonates at a personal level in a way that technological and domain-specific solutions never will. Telling the right security story also aligns the strategic functions of the CISO with the core business objectives of other executives in a way that invites active collaboration from the very same people who would otherwise say "no" if they couldn't see a direct, near-term, and tangible benefit.

4
Don't Call Me Sue

I am working with the newly hired Director of Security at this PaaS provider. A sharp, witty, hilarious fellow who is destined to become a very good friend in the future.

We don't know that yet.

Together, we have been going over the risky practices I had already discovered, and the ones he managed to flush out in his first "official" week. It's a veritable train wreck. Some of the issues are downright frightening, and I don't scare easily.

Today, however, we are engaging in one of my favorite security management techniques, if you can call it that; we are meeting with the general counsel.

At hand is an item that stuck out like a sore thumb to us, out of a literal list of hundreds. The issue is data retention. Specifically, the company's practice of preserving transactional data—including credit card accounts—indefinitely because "customers like to search transaction history."

The general counsel is receptive. He's bright, and between him and the security director, the conversation flows easily, with plenty of comments to crack us all up at times.

After providing the necessary background, we get to the problem. "You see," I tell counsel, "from a risk perspective, you are preserving the liability of every account you keep for as long as you keep it."

"Right," he says.

"Well, that adds up to two things: your cyberinsurance premiums are probably higher than they would be otherwise, and it is more likely that a breach will result in enough uncovered

DOI: 10.1201/9781003302759-8

losses that it increases the chance the business will not be able to sustain them."

His eyes light up. "That I fully get. Thank you for speaking my language."

"Here is the challenge we're facing, though," I continue. "The marketing folks are convinced that your customers would depart posthaste should this change. I'm usually pretty good at breaking these logjams, but here we need your help."

Over the next few weeks, we work with him and the VP of Marketing to craft a new approach. We take it upon ourselves to speak to the larger, more strategic customers, and eventually settle on the idea that, while the company will continue to maintain transaction history indefinitely, credit card account numbers will be limited to 30 days by default. Customers who insist on longer storage must sign an additional liability waiver.

They can always get the card numbers from their processor, anyway.

Not a single customer seems to mind. Heck, a couple of them even thank us for being extra vigilant on their behalf. The platform change itself occurs over the next quarter. The number of customers that insist we do things the way we did before and sign the waiver? A big, fat zero.

The number we lose over the change? Same.

And counsel? In one of our meetings about a year later, he tells me this: "You know, Barak, I want to tell you something about that thing we did with the credit cards. I don't want you to feel bad about all the rest of the amazing work you're doing with us, but I truly believe that this was the most effective technology risk reduction change we have ever implemented in this company."

He pauses reflectively for a moment, then adds, "And it didn't cost us a penny!"

The company's top lawyer is the quintessential support function. They are not there to generate new business, but rather to ensure that the organization does not make costly decisions that could ultimately harm its operations to an unsustainable degree.

In other words, they are the ultimate risk managers.

Sounds familiar?

Arguably, the CISO's most critical role is that of risk manager, albeit in a different context; instead of refereeing commercial liability, their role is focused on the risk inherent in the use of technology and, even more critically, data. Their training is highly specialized—just like the corporate counsel's—although often less formal. As a result, your typical security leader has a uniquely valuable view of the various risks that are present in everyday business operations.

When it comes to handling technology risk in contracts, this neatly intersects with the general counsel's role. And these days, technology risk and liability is the hidden monster lurking in the contract closet (née clauses).

To illustrate, let me share with you the "top-3 list of things where SaaS vendors and legal processes collide," alternatively called the "things that make no sense in the cloud world":

- *The Right to Audit Clause.* This is the seemingly innocent requirement, present in practically every enterprise contract, which allows the customer to audit the vendor upon request (or at any time) if the former suspects that the latter is not doing what they are supposed to be doing or, ah, speaking out of both sides of their mouth.

  No problem so far, right?

  Well, let me ask you something.

  If your company runs in the public cloud (e.g. AWS, Google, Azure), and you do not even have access to the facilities yourself, how would you deal with an incoming request from your customer to audit those facilities?

  The problem with this clause is that it assumes that the vendor is in control of its technical infrastructure, an assumption that is rapidly becoming obsolete as companies move more and more of their backoffice and production operations into the care of abstracted, virtual entities (at least from the perspective of technology infrastructure operations). For the vendor to sign this clause is, effectively, to break the contract at the moment of execution, since it is clear that such a promise or attestation *cannot be made in good faith.*

- Yet how many contracts are out there with this clause? Hundreds of thousands? Millions? If you're in legal, on either side of this line, how truly comfortable are you knowing that there is a clause in the contract that, by its very definition, can never be satisfied?

- We already discussed the solution to this one earlier; all it requires is for the customer to reframe the clause to exclude the right as it pertains to these kinds of cloud facilities. But then we go back to liability, and representation of the "behind the scenes" public cloud by the vendor as captured in the contract, and... it can get a little tricky if not carefully handled.

- *The Security Policy Clause.* If ever there was a stupid legal notion advanced by security practitioners, it is the idea that they can force their services vendors to comply with specific security policies.

  Yes, you heard me right. Stupid.

  Idiotic. Utterly moronic. Dumb as fuck.*

  Assuming my publisher let this last bit slide... am I being clear enough?

  If you are doing this, then I ask that you stop. Stop now. Tell your legal department that this clause needs to be rewritten, pronto. Then keep reading.

  Here is why it has to stop: your vendor can *never make such an attestation in good faith and remain in business.*

  There are several problems here. I'll ignore all but two of them, which can be summarized thusly: "policies are living documents" and...

  Actually, now that I think of it, let's just keep it to that one.

  Policies are living documents.

  See, each company has its own unique set of business circumstances. If it takes security even half seriously, then its security policies will reflect the nature of its business and its specific constraints and will continue to do so as it evolves. If

---

* Urban Dictionary states that "dumb as fuck" is "One of the only grammatical instances where the word 'fuck' cannot be used." That pretty much sums up my feeling about security policies in contracts.

that company is your vendor, this is precisely *what you want and hope for*.

Policies change often, by design.

Contracts very rarely change, also by design.

Square peg and round hole, anyone? We're already off to a really bad start.

Now you try to also force the vendor into a straightjacket of policies that reflect the priorities and realities of your business at (roughly) the specific moment that the contract was signed.

How does this make any sense at all?

Not only that, but the vendor is also supposed to follow your company's policies in the future, even while they also change.

Policies that may make no sense in the vendor's operational environment.

Policies that could quite literally drive bad security practices when considered in the context of their business environment.

Policies that will conflict with policies that other customers like you are forcing them to adhere to, resulting in a total breakdown of their entire policy infrastructure. That is, if they even attempt to actually follow anybody's requirements, which they don't, because *it doesn't make any friggin' sense*, contracts be damned.

Here, let me pick on another well-known giant to illustrate. Figure 4.1 is part of Yahoo's contract requirements from its service vendors at the time of this writing (https://policies.yahoo.com/us/en/yahoo/terms/vendor/networksecuritysaas/index.htm, version 3/25/2013, which was shockingly **still current** as of 11/15/2022).

This is laughable.

First, why insist on passwords at all? The world of security is constantly trying to move away from them, and for good reasons.

But the truly astonishing part is the term "reasonably complex." What does that mean, in a legal sense?

2.3. Access Control.

a. Vendor will permit access to The System only to authorized persons on a need-to-know-basis.

b. The System, excluding physical premises, will at all times be protected by an authentication system that complies with the following requirements: (i) **passwo**rds will be reasonably complex; (ii) use of privileged

---

Figure 4.1 Excerpt from Yahoo's contract requirements from its service vendors.

c. Encryption.

i. Where data must be encrypted under the terms of these Network Security Terms, other parts of the Agreement, or Laws, Vendor will sign and encrypt using a Yahoo-approved algorithm. The following algorithms are pre-approved by Yahoo: (a) 3DES, (b) AES, (c) RSA-1024bit+, (d) HMAC-SHA-1, and (e) The MD5-based signature scheme used for Yahoo APIs as described on http://developer.yahoo.com, as such scheme may be independently updated by Yahoo from time to time. All other algorithms must be specifically approved by Yahoo's security team in writing prior to use and will be subject to any limitations prescribed by Yahoo in its approval.

Figure 4.2 Excerpt from Yahoo service agreement.

Let me answer this question for you:

It has no meaning.

Why is it even there? Who allowed that to happen and how did it make it through legal review?

Do you get the sense that Yahoo security and Yahoo legal are not exactly on super-friendly terms?

A little earlier in the same agreement is the gem shown in Figure 4.2 (available online).

We deserve a moment of levity, so let me ask this: why on earth would any vendor's security team trust that the Yahoo security team—responsible for one of the largest breaches in the history of the world—to come up with any sort of reasonable encryption standard?

OK, I'm not being fair. The truth is that no security posture can ever resist a determined, skilled attacker forever, especially not one that is sponsored by a state actor. But the Yahoo hack is incidentally useful as an examination of the potential impact of security on the business. In this case, it cost the Yahoo shareholders $350M dollars in the Verizon bid. Not a trivial sum.

But back to our topic. Even if they were, say, Google's vaunted security team—again, why on earth should they be dictating this? There are perfectly good sources for obtaining this sort of thing from, like NIST, which publishes updated encryption and key management standards regularly. Why not simply agree to follow those instead? BlueKrypt maintains a great free resource summarizing this stuff: www.keylength.com/. Why not just state that "both parties agree to adhere to NIST standards," or some such?

It would sure make things easier, cleaner, clearer, and ultimately more secure, because all parties know what is expected of them now and in the future, and there is a common and simple understanding that has actual, enforceable legal meaning.

All this policy in contract stuff is silly. You know this. The vendor knows this. So why insist on pretending otherwise?

I'll tell you why. It's called laziness, and it's inexcusable.

Here is what we all need to do: decide, internally, which established published security standards we are willing to accept as assurances of a proper security program and methodology.

You may settle on various combinations, say, PCI and SOC2 or maybe CSA-Star and ISO. Whatever makes you happy. The most common combo these days is ISO27001+SOC2, and it's a damn good one.

There is no one thing that works for everyone, so I strongly recommend you create a menu of sorts to guide the evaluation efforts by your business managers and, if you have them, your regulators.

Craft your replacement clause to require that the vendor follows these established standards as they also evolve, and that they provide you with validation on a recurring basis (say, annually) that they are doing so. Preferably, such validation will be performed by an external independent party (also known as "an auditor"), but it doesn't have to be; it's up to you and the specific business case and scenario in question.

Then remove every single shred of prescriptive security policy requirements from your contracts. They don't matter. They *shouldn't* matter; a good agreed-upon set of established standards will dictate those controls so you don't have to do it yourself. There are, after all, some very clever folks working on these standards and evolving them for you!

Trust me: you do not want to appear in court to argue a security policy item after a breach. Trial lawyers may be excited by this notion, but security folks and general counsels generally have better things to do with their time.

Although to be fair, having been named as an expert witness in such situations, I'll admit that the side income can be pretty good.

- *The Subcontractor Clause.* This one is a little more subtle. The clause here is one that is often driven by regulation—say, if your company (or agency) is subject to Department of Defense (DoD) rules. But like in many other walks of life, there can be too much of a good thing, and thankfully, DoD rules do not apply to that many organizations—and even when they do, some leeway can be had if scoping is considered carefully.

  But back to basics. What is this clause? Essentially, it's the one that requires that vendors obtain preapproval from the customer whenever a "subcontractor" is added to the team.

  Here is how this proposition increasingly runs into a serious problem: for many technology—and especially cloud—vendors, the entire company is virtualized. Their headquarters are nothing more than a glorified coffee shop, with wireless Internet access and, quite literally, no local infrastructure anywhere.

  They simply don't manage anything directly.

  Not even a network.

  In this kind of environment, "subcontractors" are a way of life—they can get added and removed daily, without much notice or, for that matter, particular care. Accounting wishes to sign up and use an analytics tool for sales trending reports? They can do so on their own without even going through IT, let alone a procurement process. If one actually attempts to audit cloud-based subcontractors (in the form of SaaS tools) in these environments, one will often discover that there are hundreds of them in use at any given time. Part of the attraction is precisely that they are so easy to add and discard.

  Heck, it's such a rapidly evolving field that there are already some excitingly valuable startups in Silicon Valley built around just keeping track in real time of what services people are using. Just this one thing!

  In other words, it is literally impossible for that vendor to legitimately make the promise that they will request approval from any one customer for every such change, let alone many customers.

  Of course, one obvious way to narrow down the clause is by limiting this requirement to subcontractors that are part of the service delivery environment, or in simpler terms, those that touch the vendor's software that is used by the customer.

But delve deeper and you'll see that this is also an unrealistic proposition. In a world where people tout ideas like "no-ops" and everything is abstracted sixteen ways from next Tuesday, development teams constantly add hook-ins to various cloud APIs. The entire world of technology services is about "moving business at the speed of light," or something like that. The very expectation that a vendor would even remember to notify the customer and request permission for every such change, let alone choose to do so and delay their deployment cycle by weeks at a time, is silly.

The truth is that we're really all just pretending. Nobody actually reaches out to each and every enterprise customer to ask for permission before adding some new tech in engineering.

So let's narrow this further. How about we limit the clause to just human subcontractors? Now we're getting somewhere. But it's still inelegant; after all, technology subcontractors (like developers) are often working from remote locations, under sub-entities established in target countries, and trying to figure out which kind of employee triggers a requirement for permission and which does not is, in the best case, incredibly difficult.

Yet, there is one thing we seem to be ignoring in this discussion. Often, these vendors provide—yes, you guessed it—an abstraction layer. Their product, virtual as it may be, is in one cloud (say, GitHub), whereas the service layer is in another (such as AWS), the customer's specific service environment in a third (like an individual VPC), and the customer's data is in a fourth (a specific S3 bucket, maybe).

And any vendor with a decent security program—which we can check, say, via examination of their security framework as attested to in audit reports by external auditors—will have a very strong role segregation control with a very, very small group of people that could even theoretically access customer data. This is a beneficial side effect of the very nature of how they run their business. It's part of the tradeoff for them. *When you lose control of the infrastructure, you inevitably end up compensating at the access layer.*

As a side note, do you remember the discussion we had about the "invisible NOC"? If so, then what I am about to suggest is probably obvious, which is to actually try and understand these operating models. It is entirely possible that the only subcontractors that matter are the people in the DevOps team, and a legal clause requiring that only they have access and that notification is required for these subcontractors with access is a much stronger one than the typical, overly-broad, impossible-to-follow "everyone."

If nothing else, it's much easier to enforce or otherwise prove deficient/negligent when things go bad.

The above are the top three issues that I always look for in contracts between EAmmune's cloud-based technology vendor clients and their enterprise customers. Addressing these issues contractually is difficult, and it becomes impossible if nobody is there to identify them. And it's the kind of thing that only comes back to haunt you at the worst possible moment.

When working with legal counsel, a good CISO will need the skills of a paralegal and the eagerness of a courtroom advocate. But just like with the sales VP, corporate counsel is a relationship to be fostered, not ignored. Both roles are in high-trust positions. Both deal with risk management. Both are often making decisions that are potentially far-reaching, yet with impacts that remain invisible in the short term and, with any luck, the long term as well. These two jobs are so complimentary that I argue often that a CISO might as well at least report to counsel via dotted line.

Just like we did with sales and marketing, we can try to list the main direct contributions that a CISO can bring to legal. These would be the following:

- *Identifying Hidden Liabilities.* Liability caps are standard practice, but what if they do not cover or explicitly exclude reasonably likely events? Sometimes, it is simply a matter of understanding technology and data risk enough to visualize the scenario. A common example refers to data protection. Many customers understandably insist that their vendors protect their data at all times, and safely remove it upon termination. But what if the vendor, say, doesn't have physical control or even access to the underlying media, because their product is deployed in the cloud? Unless the customer's counsel has seen this before, they would not be aware that a standard clause requiring that the vendor securely erase customer data and provide proof of such is (for the most part) *technically impossible to deliver*. And yet, such a clause is often executed because it appears normal. It could easily be brought up in litigation.

- *Avoiding Risky Clauses and Negotiating More Sensible Ones Instead.* The most common offender here is, as we discussed above, the issue of security policy compliance. One of the most common errors we observe in enterprise contracts as they pertain to security is the misguided attempt to specify precise technical controls. These are often enumerated in some form of "data protection" appendix. The issue here is that security is a rapidly evolving field. Therefore, committing to specific controls may not only be extremely difficult to follow (from the vendor's perspective, and especially across multiple contracts), and impossible to enforce in practice (from the customer's perspective, and especially across multiple vendors). Worse, such specificity may harm security in the long term. Let's look at passwords again; they are, in general, a poor access control mechanism. Password standards are often misunderstood and poorly applied and must evolve to deal with the ever-increasing capabilities of attackers. The security world is increasingly moving away from passwords as a primary access control method. Yet, many contracts enshrine the use of "7-character" passwords (yes, seven!) as a minimum requirement for security, for eternity, and forever. That is, charitably, laughable as a security measure, does not hold the vendor to task at all, and allows them to get away with seriously bad practices. And the only reason this happened in the first place is that the CISO who helped "draft" that contract just wanted to get legal out of their hair. Let's not delude ourselves that they will remember to approach legal in order to trigger the process of reopening all their contracts to renegotiate this clause at some time in the future (are you smiling?). Just like in the case of security policy, it is much better to enforce a common, established, and evolving standard for access control security, and agree that the vendor continues to follow that standard over time.
- *Harmonizing Master Services Agreements (MSAs).* Oh boy. If you've been in the field for any serious length of time, you will

have seen this phenomenon: vendors signing different MSAs with different clients that, at some point, start conflicting with each other. I am, of course, still discussing security here; this does happen in other areas, although less often. Security, however, has only recently made it into the world of legal and contractual liability in a big way, and it is therefore in a bit of a Wild West state in this regard. To build on the last point, think of the MSA that promises one company to comply with a data protection standard postulated in appendix F of that contract, and another company to comply with one in appendix C of another contract . . . except when those two standards are put next to each other, which they almost never are, they are not compatible, and they may even conflict directly. Even if someone manages to catch this conflict, which is a highly dubious proposition, how would the vendor resolve this issue internally? By building two separate environments with different control sets for each one? Not only is this an open liability, but it also serves to reduce the overall effectiveness of the security program, because when too much of this happens, "everything legal" becomes meaningless to security, who end up doing their own thing and treating legal as an occasionally unpleasant interruption. Not to mention that operationally, this kind of setup is practically impossible to manage well consistently, over time.

Isn't it better to have direct ongoing security involvement in the crafting of MSAs so that this issue doesn't even arise in the first place? And to those of you who are in security who just had an "Ah-ha!" moment: I will gently remind you to train yourself to work with legal on *their* terms, not yours.

- *Knowing What to Watch Out For.* Legal will, in reality, often reach out to the security team to ask for help with respect to signing up with third parties. There are actually two distinct sub-elements here. The smaller (although critical) aspect is knowing which requirements to apply to the company's vendors. For example, does any particular vendor fall within the scope of a particular rule or regulation? While the easiest and most conservative answer is "sure!," that can frustrate the business, present obstacles to productivity growth, and ultimately lead to internal resentment toward the CISO, a sadly all-too-typical career-blocker. The second, and arguably more significant element, is in answering the question of how to apply the company's internal risk posture toward vendor management and acquisition. As we discussed, one way NOT to do it is—all together now—by forcing vendors to agree to abide by the company's security policies. Another, which we touched upon earlier, is via a mammoth RFP/questionnaire designed to address "security frameworks," which are often largely inappropriate for the vendor in question and is really just another form of enshrining policy in contract. Now expand the above into the world of customers and partners and clashing priorities . . . is it Friday yet?

Speaking of RFPs, there is another hidden danger inherent in the security RFP process beyond the fallacy of "one size fits all." If moved out of the realm of due diligence and into a legal context, as some companies are increasingly doing, RFPs can be interpreted in one of two ways. Either it is a point-in-time self-assessment, which means that the responses are essentially no more than a vague assertion that carries no real weight behind it ("this is what it was like at the time I answered this question"), or it is a contractual artifact implying a legal commitment. And by treating it as the latter, we are back where we started; security postures change and evolve, while contracts, once executed, tend to gather dust. Thus, if your legal team does this, or if you are in legal and are using security RFPs as contractual addendums, I again beg of you—stop. Find a better way.

Let security perform validation and report back with risk-based conclusions. Work together to assess risk in context. Legal and security both understand risk well within their respective domains.

It should be a cinch!

And it should be plenty.

4.2
ORANGE COVERALL BLUES

In discussing the intersection of security and legal, a new kind of complication has arisen in 2022, which is the real risk of the security leader ending up in jail.

To recap: Joe Sullivan, the CISO at Uber, was indicted and then convicted on two federal charges. The first was obstructing an FTC investigation, and the other was misprision, or concealing a felony.

These charges were filed after it came to light that, during an active FTC incident into a previous breach at the company, Uber was informed by an external group of hackers that they managed to again make their way into sensitive Uber data systems. As the CISO and in charge of incident response, Joe did two charge-inducing things.

First, he directed the hackers to Uber's bug bounty program. A bug bounty program is a way in which companies can invite hackers to try and hack their systems, report their findings, and get monetary awards for those findings. It's an important tool in the CISO's arsenal, and one that every leading technology company like Uber relies upon in order to improve their cybersecurity efforts. This normal-looking action led to the misprision charge.

Then, in subsequent discussions with the FTC, when asked if there was anything new to report in connection to the previous breach they were investigating, Joe failed to disclose the interaction with the hackers. This action led to the obstruction charge.

There are plenty of news stories in the media on this case if you wish to check it out further, but none of them touch on the internal intersection between security and legal.

Let's see if we can do that here.

First of all, I feel for Joe. Even the judge, during pretrial motions, noted dryly that it seemed like Joe was on trial for the entire Uber corporation. There are certainly elements of this trial that hint at the possibility of extrajudicial agendas. One is that Joe, who used to be an assistant United States attorney (read: federal prosecutor), should have known better than many of his peers in the space. Or more darkly, the notion that the prosecutor tried to turn Joe against the really big fish—one Travis Kalanick, CEO of Uber, who was deeply involved and called some of the important shots about the breach—but Joe wouldn't turn.

You could read speculative articles about this until your eyes bleed. It's the kind of thing that makes TV show producers squeal. Who knows, a show might even be made between the time I write this and when the book is published.

But let's talk about how this stuff happens behind the scenes. Having served as CISO for so many companies, I've been in the hot seat around incidents, like the one Uber experienced that led to this trial, more times than you have fingers and toes.

Let's do it in the form of Q&A.

First Question: Is it a Breach?

Unless you're the kind of CISO that shouldn't be a CISO, you never make decisions about whether an incident is a breach or not (the "*key question*"). It's not your job. It's never your job. You know whose job it is? Corporate counsel. One interesting feature of Joe's team was that he actually had counsel in his team, reporting to him, to answer this *key question*. This is not typical in security departments! Presumably, Joe's prior experience in law enforcement led him to make an advanced hire. Unfortunately for him, said lawyer (Craig Clark) ended up state's witness, after being turned by the prosecutor in the case.

This added an unusual dimension to the case. Were Joe operating in a more typical corporate security environment, he would have had to reach out to general counsel for the *key question*. By having his own breach counsel, Joe effectively insourced the responsibility for the *key question*, and *became accountable to it* as that lawyer's boss. This is a critical nuance. If you're a CISO and want an immediate takeaway, I would tell you to learn from Joe's experience, and never, ever allow a lawyer to be part of your team. Let general counsel and their team own the determination around breach notifications, as it is very much within their job description, and very much not within yours.

Does that feel oppositional? Perhaps. But keep in mind that general counsel is the company's lawyer and as such, has certain protections built into their role that the CISO does not. It also keeps things where they belong, with the CISO informing and advising about the nature of the incident, and counsel managing the legal and regulatory implications. The CISO should have (and share!) an opinion, but the lawyer whose job is to know the law (duh), gets to determine whether any legal requirements arise from the incident and importantly, the *key question*: whether it qualifies as a breach.

It's an important lesson, I think.

At least, as CISO, you wouldn't be the only person standing trial.

Second Question: Should you Ever Override Counsel's Decision?

Ultimately, this is the real impact of this trial. If we are to follow the narrative, it goes something like this: CISOs are now going to be a lot more inclined to act as whistle-blowers around security incidents, because they would be afraid of the orange jumpsuit. What incentive would they have to act other than extremely conservatively? In turn, companies are going to hate the people in this role even more than they do right now. You think CISOs are difficult to work with today? How everyone wishes they could think more in terms of being business enablers instead of fear merchants?

Oh, just you wait.

Unfortunately, none of this is good for the practice of security in an organization. But, as always, there are many glossed-over nuances here. For example, if general counsel (remember the first point above) writes to the CISO saying "we do not believe this is a breach and it does not require notification," then the CISO's ass is covered. It is, yes. Take a deep breath. It is. You know why? Because the CISO didn't hire corporate counsel and counsel doesn't work for the CISO. So if the regulator, say the FTC, claims the CISO neglected to inform them of something, it's a different story if the legal opinion driving the action doesn't come from the CISO's own lawyer that reports directly to them.

In the legal context, this stuff matters.

I can't pretend to know what sort of internal pressures Joe was facing in terms of that FTC disclosure, by the way. But I imagine that nobody at Uber wanted additional embarrassment at that point in the company's life, leading into an IPO and all that jazz. It's one of the most galling aspects of this entire case, because even without knowing anything, I bet that Mr. Kalanick (Founder of Uber and CEO at the time) felt quite strongly about not talking to the FTC about it.

As for the method Joe used to "hide" the breach; here I must laugh. Let's be clear about this: there are no "black hats" and "white hats." There are only "gray hats." If funnelling a disclosure to a bug bounty program with the partial and explicit goal of getting the vulnerability reporters under NDA is a felony, then by all means, come arrest me now; I've made this recommendation quite literally hundreds of times. It's a big part of bug bounty programs, the arm's length aspect that allows us to keep an ever more complex technology environment in a more or less reasonably secure shape so the company can conduct its business. If everything was always made public immediately, as appears to be the righteous position taken by the prosecutor in this case, then companies simply could not function due to the constant barrage of security priorities, and their only option would be the discontinue their bug bounty programs, directly leading to significant harm of their cyber posture.

I can't imagine anyone thinks this is a good idea for data protection. Not even the regulators.

Third Question: At $100,000, was it an Unusually Large Bounty and Didn't that Indicate Some Shady Intentions to Illegally Hide Stuff?

Sure, it was a lot. But the payment fit the disclosure. It wasn't out of line in that sense; from what I could learn from the trial information, and based on my experience in this area, anything up to a quarter million or so would have been reasonable. So kudos to Joe's team for negotiating a reduced payment with the hackers.

Much more importantly, Uber bought not just an NDA, but a certification of data destruction. That's pretty good, and while of course you can't ensure that the person on the other side isn't lying to you (and lying isn't a crime), at the very least it looks like Uber, through Joe, attained the best possible outcome with respect to this incident.

Incidents happen! And let me tell you, no one likes to make them public. Been there, done that, and companies, through counsel (just not your counsel, CISOs), will always choose not to notify the public if they have reasonable legal grounds to avoid the notification. That in itself does not implicate anyone in a crime, not even the person nominally tasked with trying to prevent incidents from happening.

Or it should not, anyway.

And yes, the issue of whether Joe had a legal obligation to tell the regulator (FTC) about it is of course essential. Reading between the lines, it comes down to a group of people (Joe, Travis the CEO, Craig the Lawyer, et al.) convincing themselves that it wasn't necessary because they were afraid of what it might do to Uber's IPO prospects. To then single Joe out for this decision seems preposterous. If you want to charge them, then charge all of them. That's exactly what the judge noted in pretrial motions, and why Craig was offered immunity from prosecution in return for burning his boss. Take from this what you will.

Fourth Question. Does this Change the Role of the CISO itself as a Company Officer?

Took me long enough.

It's a tough one. From my perspective, it definitely gives CISOs a reason for pause. Here is where I think that my perspective might help: as a perennial vCISO, I'm never an employee, let alone an officer, so all I can do is recommend; there is never a question of me making a decision about the *key question*. It's never my decision. In a way, it might work well for full-time CISOs to take that approach as well.

In a world where the real possibility of facing criminal charges for simply doing your job as CISO is a thing, there might be benefit to refocusing one's approach towards the more advisory side of things. Less authoritarian, more collaborative. There is a maturity element to this. Many CISOs tend to think that their job is more important than it really is—I did write a book about it, after all (this one, ha)—and this case may provide a bit of a reality check. Joe is smart, and charismatic, and a leader. The problem arises when the role is then cast in this mold.

Because it's very easy to believe that, as CISO, you are the "protector of the company," and demand the matching decision-making authority.

Here is the thing: people will happily let you do just that.

Do you know why?

Because when you fail, then you own the responsibility for it.

And the matching orange jump suit.

5

COMPLY OH MY

It is time to turn our attention to everyone's absolutely favorite topic—security compliance.

I can faintly hear that grunt of satisfaction even as you settle happily in your chair.

It seems that, increasingly, there is no single more effective tool in the CISO's arsenal to utilize in getting projects funded than by raising the spectre of potential non-compliance.

It's the WMD of Information Security.

CEOs and boards are increasingly finding themselves with a rising and quaintly conflicting sense that

1 Their business is at risk from an ever-increasing threat that they do not understand.
2 The person telling them this—be they the CISO, the compliance manager, or whomever else owns this "thing"—is clearly overstating their case.

Sounds familiar?

This leads to a polarization of sorts. One has to publicly trust one's compliance people, after all. At the same time, one is not entirely unhappy to see the compliance people pay a high price when the inevitable failure occurs. It's the whole slipping on a banana peel sentiment. It's terrible but, uhh, hella funny. That is because security, as we have been demonstrating throughout this book, can only be a winning game if it is reconsidered as something other than a constant battle of wits between two opposing clubs, and one where the odds are highly skewed against the home team.

There are good solutions to this problem, which we will cover in our concluding chapter, but for now, let's get back to focusing on the issue

DOI: 10.1201/9781003302759-10

of compliance. Our first goal will be to deconstruct security compliance as much as we can.

Hold on, this will take a while.

Sorry. But it has to be done.

First, there are several realms of security compliance.

U.S. (or International) Federal Regulations for Private Industry: Here, we refer to laws like SOX, GLBA, and HIPAA, and, specifically, to the portions within those laws that drive data security controls. As one might expect, while the regulations themselves are far-reaching in terms of their impact on targeted industries, they are also, for the most part, widely open to interpretation when it comes to actual control design and implementation. They are not prescriptive. For example, SOX 404 cares about the integrity of financial reporting and the underlying financial systems, but it does not explicitly specify how to ensure such integrity or, indeed, measure the effectiveness of related security implementations; it is up to the auditor to identify the various critical (or key) controls. This can be a lucrative business, and it is worth remembering that the auditor actually carries a modicum of personal accountability in this particular arena and thus has no incentive to be anything but highly conservative in their approach. Yet, we often see environments where key controls overlap (leading to waste and operational fatigue) or worse, make no sense at all from a data security perspective. For instance, consider HiTrust, a standard designed to address the issue of compliance with the data security elements in HIPAA. HiTrust takes an all-or-nothing approach with respect to its interpretation of the HIPAA rules and then goes further in applying security controls that are not only counterintuitive but may be damaging to a company's security posture. For example, HiTrust requires that administrators rotate their passwords every 60 days—an approach that even NIST has discarded as ineffective and ultimately harmful. From our experience, attempting to get the HiTrust folks to accept an alternative control—such as using multichannel authentication (or, heaven forbid, passwordless authentication)—will generally fall on deaf ears. Similarly, they require that anti-malware is deployed on each and every computing device, whether it makes sense or not; a hardened Linux box will generally not benefit from running anti-virus unless it happens to be a mail or file server, and nor would an environment where the end-user PC population is truly segregated and runs on completely different classes of operating systems from production (which is often the case in cloud-native environments). This leads to absurd compromises, such as the mass deployment of ClamAV on Linux servers, an utterly useless control that enables the organization to "check the box" but does nothing other than add an unnecessary package to a Puppet manifest.* This is a bad practice, since one of the principles of good security is to never have more on the machine than you absolutely need to have. This is because every software element introduces the potential for more security vulnerabilities—yes, even security software. The fact that a piece of software is designed to function in a security role does not mean that it is written securely! (the compromise of RSA Secure-ID stands out here, or that little thing that happened with Solarwinds)

Some federal regulations can have a larger impact. For example, privacy rules such as the Children's Online Privacy Protection Act (COPPA) impact any company that provides services, and engages in electronic marketing, to children under 13 years of age (Ed-Tech is an industry often dealing with COPPA issues). As a result of the burdens of satisfying COPPA rules, many large online platforms simply avoid offering their services to the younger set, which has to qualify as a fairly significant regulatory impact. But the United States has still not passed any comprehensive privacy laws with respect to consumer privacy, relying instead on a mishmash of state laws; the CCPA—California Consumer Privacy Act—is the leading one. This means that U.S. domestic companies tend to operate in a looser environment, and that leads to complacency in handling sensitive consumer information.

How many U.S. domestic companies do you know that actually have mechanisms to, say, encrypt consumer PII beyond credit card account numbers?

If there is one crystal clear way to show the foundational difference between the United States and the EU in handling consumer privacy

---

* If this isn't meaningful to you, briefly, every computer runs a bunch of software, which is made of components called *packages*, such as an anti-virus software package. Puppet is the name of a popular piece of software that typically manages the configurations of a large number of computers. A Puppet manifest is, in part, the list of packages that get installed on each of those managed computers.

rights, it must be in the "opting" mechanism. The EU is an "opt-in" regime—for a company to market to a consumer, that consumer must take action in order to have that happen. The United States is an "opt-out" regime—for a consumer to avoid marketing from a company, they must take action to make it stop.

It really is an entirely different way of looking at things. And the implications can be profound.

International Privacy Regulations: The world, and the EU in particular, has increasingly drafted rules for the protection of their residents' PII. The EU's is the General Data Protection Regulation (GDPR). A unified set of rules about privacy that applies to any company operating within EU borders, the GDPR can have a dramatic effect in terms of compliance and includes robust penalties (up to 4% of total *global revenue*) that can be levied against companies that fail to follow those rules.

Oh, and one of those rules? Formal appointment of a Data Protection Officer (DPO). Let me put it this way: you think CISOs are commanding high salaries now? I'll leave it as an exercise to the reader to figure out the growth in market value of a good CISO with a proven understanding of privacy issues. It certainly hasn't slowed at all since I first wrote this bit.

Considering the potential fines, if you happen to be a multinational company with presence in the EU, your CISO better understand not just your technology operations but your business operations really, *really* well.

U.S. Government Rules: Trickier than either of the above categories are rules required of any vendor wanting to work with U.S. government agencies. Those agencies are bound by FISMA/FedRAMP rules, and in some cases, DoD regulations.

An example of such regulation? Non-U.S. citizens are prohibited from working on, around, near, or for that matter breath the same air (and not because of COVID-19) as those U.S. citizens who do work on the platform providing the services in question.

Maybe I'm exaggerating a wee bit. But not by much.

I don't know if you've heard, but turns out that the world is chock-full of incredibly smart and talented people who work in technology, and—I know this is going to come as a major shock—do not, in fact, possess American citizenship. Many of them are in the United States working for those companies that are the most innovative in the world and provide the most value with their products and services.

Or—who knows?—they might be working from a remote office (note: three years into the COVID-19 pandemic, I feel lucky for having written this suggestion way back when).

Figuring this one out is beyond the scope of this book, as it involves politics as much as anything. But it is one major reason behind the apparent inability of U.S. government agencies to catch up with the times, technologically speaking.

State Rules: I have a little story to share here.

I'm sitting in the office of the city's CIO. It's a big California city, and this guy actually knows his stuff, which unfortunately can sometimes be rare in these settings.

We're talking about security efforts and what can work in his highly limited budgetary constraints, when I bring up SB1386 compliance.

His eyes lock on me as he gives me that look. You know, that mixture of apathy and empathy which can mean that you either: (1) said something really, really stupid; or (2) have peed yourself in public. I quickly check my pants. No such luck.

"Why did you call it that?" he asks me in a patronizing tone.

"Ah . . . call who what now? Umm . . ." I sound dumber by the moment. Honestly, I have no clue what I did. I thought we were having fun.

"SB1386. Why did you call it that?" he demands again.

"Well, because that's what it's called . . . I mean . . ." I begin to welter under his gaze, "isn't it?"

"No!" he states emphatically. "It most certainly is not called that."

He gives me a few seconds to stew, then out of the blue, he laughs. I'm so rattled that I forget to smile.

"I was just giving you a hard time, man. But you shouldn't call it that anymore, because it's a law now. You know what SB stands for, right?"

That light bulb over my head finally flickers to life. Thank you, Edison. Took you long enough.

"Senate bill . . . it's a law now, so it's no longer a bill. I got you."

This conversation happened in the Naughties when the revisions to the law (the 1977 California Information Practices Act [CIPA]) based on that senate bill passed, when it was still a pretty big deal. Amusingly enough, people continued to refer to it as SB1386, right until the CCPA came along.

Due to the lack of comprehensive federal rules, the United States is essentially a mess, domestically, with different rules in different states. Considering that domestic U.S. companies operating online tend to serve the entire United States, every single one of them is bound by a rather mystifying array of rules and regulations that, truth be told, most of them never even heard about, let alone tried to address.

I'm fairly certain there is significant money to be made by an enterprising lawyer who decides to start applying these rules to the myriad of United States-based companies doing domestic business. Ambulance chasers are an honored American tradition (turns out I was right here, too; those class actions have started and the pace is rising).

Industry Standards: By far, the most successful and well-known program in this arena is the Payment Card Industry Data Security Standard, or PCI-DSS (PCI for short). An evolution of other data protection standards such as the British Security standard (BS7799), PCI has become a de facto standard of data protection in many industries. Often enough, this is true even in environments that bear little or no relationship to credit card security. PCI confers a couple of major advantages: (1) being prescriptive, [†] it is comparatively easy to understand and implement; and (2) it has attained minor status as being a good way for service providers to communicate a reasonably established security posture to their customers.

Other well-known standards include ISO27001/2, SOC1/2/3, and CSA-Star. Each of these offers at least some level of prescriptive control sets, wide acceptance, and established auditing guidelines. They can all be useful, in the correct context, for any company that needs to demonstrate the maturity of its security program.

Keeping all of this in mind, we are now ready to move on to the next challenge.

And what might that be?

Well, we need to consider the meaning of the word "compliance."

That may come as a surprise, because everyone knows what that means, right?

No. If I may, emphatically *not so*.

Compliance is a term that is misused and abused regularly, precisely because it can be legitimately used in so many different ways and contexts.

In a nutshell, there are three general meanings to the word "compliance" that are in common use. To borrow from politics, think of them as a three-legged-stool that is absolutely necessary to be compliant in the grander sense that most of us secretly desire.

I'll use PCI to illustrate each one of them, but it works just as well for other standards:

Adherence: Here, the word "compliant" refers to the act of implementing, often on a "best effort" basis, all the relevant security controls in a particular standard or set of rules. In the PCI case, a company may be compliant (adherent) when it has evaluated internally its security posture and controls against the relevant portions of PCI, and in the company's best judgment, has applied the required controls to address any identified gaps. This is a common approach taken by vendors that sell into retail or hospitality, but do not handle credit cards directly themselves. It's also, fundamentally, the function of the Internal Audit department.

Note that one can be compliant without any sort of external review, whether formal or informal, beyond the internal process of control evaluation (or gap assessment). It can and is highly dependent on the experience and understanding of the person performing the evaluation, even if it is far from perfect.

Validation: Here, the word "compliant" means that a company has undergone some form of structured validation of its adherence to a rule or standard. This sort of assessment can take many forms, and can be internal (say, by the company's IT or Security department), or external (through an audit). In PCI, this would indicate that the company has either self-assessed its adherence to the standard (using a self-assessment questionnaire [SAQ]), or undergone an on-site assessment by a Qualified Security Assessor (QSA), resulting in a formal Report on Compliance (RoC).

The resulting compliance reports are generally called attestations (of compliance, or AoC), and in the PCI world, there is a standardized AoC format as well.

Also ... acronym heaven!

This is the normal process in the retail and hospitality spaces, but it is also common in the service provider space, where companies seek to reassure their retail and hospitality (and often banking) clients that their security program is at an acceptable level of maturity.

Other programs often provide a similar structured self-evaluation tool. For example, CSA-Star level-1 is essentially a self-assessment, just like PCI's SAQ.

Registration: Here, the word "compliant" means that there is some form of published artifact indicating that a company has adhered to a standard, was formally validated for such adherence, and has undergone a process of registration with an established authority to communicate these facts to the public. In the PCI case, each credit card association maintains its own registration program, with the most well-known being VISA's Cardholder Information Security Program [CISP].

Other programs include similar structures. For example, a HiTrust audit can be registered formally with the HiTrust Alliance (and one would be silly to embark on the process without aiming to do so); the U.S. Safe Harbor program used to allow U.S. companies to publicly attest to their privacy posture with respect to EU privacy rules, CSA-Star levels higher than 1 provide a registry, and so on.

Validated and registered compliance, as one might call this most comprehensive form, is the most helpful compliance demonstration that a company can generally exhibit. However, even then, one must be cautious. Even a public registration may not indicate proper adherence, for various reasons. For example, an attestation or registration may be based on bad audit quality. Self-assessments can sometimes be "registered," providing a fancy logo but meaning that no external validation took place. The auditor may have poor skills or be following an audit process that isn't properly designed. Some compliance shops, including surprisingly large ones, are notorious for the quality of their audits, and are known for "greenlighting compliance" as long as you pay their fee. Companies sometimes decide that it is easier to deal with the compliance audit itself instead of the underlying security posture by presenting a "happy face" to their auditors, while hiding the bad stuff. They take the approach that auditors are never paid enough to pry open all the lids in the shop, so as long as they keep the bad engines in the warehouse across the street, the one the auditors don't know about, they will be none the wiser.

These and other common problems cast a significant shadow on the entire compliance industry, and if you've ever wondered how so many massive breaches can occur when companies are "compliant," here is your answer.

If it sounds like I am contradicting myself here, since I am also encouraging customers of vendors to simply accept audit reports as an indication of security program maturity, then it is not so. All I'm saying is that one must *understand* and *accept* that there is always risk involved in working with other companies in any area, rather than assume that an audit report equals security. These are the kinds of pitfalls that exist, and instead of freaking out about them, I'm simply suggesting that folks do not pretend that some convoluted process can avoid them. It will all come together towards the end of the book, when I propose a new paradigm for thinking about security management.

Marketing departments are adept at using these terms interchangeably, under the mantle of "compliance." Thus, you will often find a vendor claiming "compliance" with a particular set of rules, but when examined more closely, the claim turns out to be that of, say, selective adherence, or maybe a self-assessment when as a client, this vendor may represent a risk that would demand external validation for an auditor. Not to mention the number of companies out there claiming all sorts of security compliance, which, when you check the fine print, means that they are in, say, the Amazon or Google cloud and are "borrowing" the cloud company compliance certifications as if they were theirs. This particular tactic still works, and often.

To add even more complexity, another area for (mis)understanding compliance is time related. Here, we again have three different adaptations, as follows:

Point-in-Time: This means that a particular company has managed to satisfy the necessary controls (i.e., adhere to a standard) at a particular point in time. It does not mean that it is compliant now, or that it was ever compliant beyond that single point in time. Amusingly, in the case of external audits and because humans cannot check everything at once, it is often the case that some controls examined earlier in the process may no longer be in place by the time controls examined later are validated. If you think about this, this essentially invalidates even the very trivial claim of ever being fully compliant at *any point in time*.

Another way to think of it is thus: what point-in-time compliance means in reality is that each control was (and possibly shown to be) adhered to at a single point in time *independently of all other controls*, during the audit window.

PCI and SOC2 type-1 are examples of (largely) point-in-time reviews.

And if you think this is rare, in deference to the Pareto rule, let me share with you that out of the hundreds of audits I have participated in, less than 20% would charitably *not* fall into this category. And I'm only referring to the ones that were successfully passed. Yes, there are always very good reasons for why things are this way. Always. Of course there are. But that doesn't change the reality, which is that many of these attested, validated audits were never strictly true, not even at a single moment in time. And lest you think I'm being persnickety, I will add that I am completely ignoring administrative (or "bureaucratic") controls, because everyone can forget to do their paperwork sometimes, and only referring to operational security ones. You know, things like patches and logs and hardening and testing and change management and all that jazz.

That said, point-in-time audits tend to be *extremely* good at identifying structural control gaps in all areas they cover, which can be very valuable information. At least if they are performed somewhat consistently.

Lookback: This is a more robust approach, taken from financial auditing, where the effectiveness of controls is examined over a period of time leading to the audit. For example, type-2 SOC2 audits will examine control effectiveness for a period of 3–12 months leading into the audit itself, requiring the organization to produce evidence showing that those controls were in fact operating successfully throughout that time.

This approach can be very helpful in terms of avoiding the main issue with point-in-time audits mentioned above, that is, the lack of adherence. If a company has to prove that its controls were working as intended for a period of time, then the chance of serious gaps in posture decreases dramatically. However, these kinds of audits tend to be impacted to a much greater degree by any issues with audit quality. Auditors who perform lookback audits must generally accept the evidence provided by their clients, who often cannot afford to fail the audit.

Then the auditors have to interpret it all correctly, and let me tell you, at least in the more nuanced aspects of any security standard review, if you show two different auditors the same set of evidence, you will receive three differing opinions.

Lookback audits, in other words, are good at identifying obvious gaps in operational control implementation, but not much else.

Look-Forward/Maturity Model: In this rarer instance, an audit attempts to assess whether the existing control map will be effective in the future. This is where frameworks (e.g., COBIT) come into play, because the only way you can assess the likelihood of the success of a control scheme is by utilizing some sort of maturity model. The concept here is simple enough. Instead of attempting to validate the existence of a control (point-in-time) or its implementation (lookback), the company's controls are graded in a standardized fashion to come up with a composite score that provides an assessment of the overall maturity of the security program. This type of audit will assess not just the existence of a particular control or its implementation, but also things like the degree to which it has been implemented.

The purpose of these kinds of audits is not to come up with a pass/ fail result (even though you typically do have minimum passing grades), but rather, to obtain a "reasonable level of confidence." They take into account the reality that a security program is often in constant motion.

The HiTrust model is a pretty good example of placing a company on the security maturity curve. However, it is directed specifically at the healthcare industry, and in my experience, skews "too rigid" in not accepting alternative or compensating controls, especially for being a maturity model. ISO27001 can provide a reasonable stand-in with respect to maturity, at least in the realm of risk governance.

The Cloud Security Alliance (CSA), with its CSA-Star program, takes a shot at combining all types of audits and frameworks into one single assessment aimed at cloud vendors. It's a (very) good effort, but by its very nature, targeted at larger organizations. A small cloud service provider, even were it sincere in its desire to both establish and demonstrate good security capabilities, would not easily be able to complete even a self-assessment CSA-Star review without hurting its growth mission. It simply takes too much time and effort to go through an audited one properly!

One last area of common misunderstanding is the difference between a "binary," or pass/fail audit, and a graded audit. The pass/fail approach is easy to explain. A list of common requirements or criteria is used, and the organization's fulfilment of each requirement is noted in yes or no fashion, or in cases where the requirement truly doesn't make sense in that particular environment, as "not-applicable." Typically, some sort of blended score, resulting from the total number of passing criteria, is assigned to a passing result, which would indicate compliance. PCI is the most widely known pass/fail audit. In the world of PCI, the only passing score is "100% of relevant requirements"— either an organization is compliant with every single requirement that is not marked "non-applicable," or it isn't. In the latter case, it is not considered to be PCI compliant.

Note the difference between 100% of *all* requirements and 100% of *relevant* requirements; it is critical to understand what a vendor feels (and their auditor agrees) is relevant to them when evaluating their security posture with respect to, say, acquiring their services. This is particularly important in any platform play, because many vendors (including Amazon/Google/Microsoft themselves as the cloud infrastructure) will sensibly limit the scope of their compliance to the backend systems they control directly to provision services on the platform. What that means in practice is that a platform may be PCI compliant, but a company utilizing the platform as a customer may at the same time not be, even if only with respect to the way they use the platform!

It is, in fact, very rare to find a platform that also offers "turnkey compliance." At one of our customers, a PaaS provider, we did just that, covering every element of PCI for not just the backend, but also for every individual customer organization, including vulnerability scans, penetration testing, WAFs, and many similar controls that platform players normally shy away from. This became an important competitive advantage but did require careful planning and strictly implemented operational guidelines across the board, as well as adoption by the leadership team at an early stage.

The graded audit model fits better in the world of frameworks, and works a bit like a risk assessment. In this case, each criteria or requirement is evaluated as an independent entity, and an attempt is made to see how well it may be designed, implemented, and maintained over time. For example, a particular control may be identified in policy, but not actually deployed. The inclusion of the control in policy indicates that a particular risk was at least considered (unless the policy was copy/pasted from public sources, an unfortunately all-too-common occurrence), even if the lack of implementation indicates a corresponding lack of attention.

The road to hell is paved with good intentions.

Similarly, an even higher score should be given when a control is monitored for effectiveness.

By evaluating each requirement or control independently, it is possible to grade the overall security posture. In the HiTrust case, for example, control requirements are grouped in categories, and each relevant requirement category must be graded as at least a "3+" on a scale of 1–5 before it is considered mature enough to pass.

Phew!

Still awake? Well done.

So now that we share a rudimentary understanding of the bewildering array of security compliance programs—stop laughing already—let's see what we can do with that, shall we?

Certain audits, especially those that are framed in a strict regulatory context, are simply things that one has to go through as part of normal operations. If you're running a public company, you will have SOX auditors crawling all over your financial reporting apparatus. If you are a healthcare organization, HIPAA is your thing. A U.S. company operating in the EU? Welcome to GDPR, NIS (Network Information Security directive, a GDPR adjunct), and a very different way of understanding and treating personally identifiable information.

A government agency?

Honestly, I feel sorry for you.

I mean it. I really do feel sorry for folks who work in government IT. For a bit of amusement, here is a cute random example of how our poor government agencies end up with the craziest IT and security implementations because of their internal compliance mandates, lack of funding, and an incredibly cumbersome onboarding process for new technologies.

This is the 2023 version of logging in to a personal treasury account for buying, selling and otherwise handling treasuries (like T-bonds). I'd say it's almost as valuable as access to a bank account. Do you notice that little phrase in parentheses? "Password is not case sensitive." This is a mainframe type of limitation from a bygone era.

Still, since they clearly couldn't invest in something even semi-modern, so they came up with an ingenious mechanism for making this limited, and frankly awkward, password-based access more, uhh, secure. Check the instructions; the only way to enter a password here is by "typing" it virtually on the "keyboard."

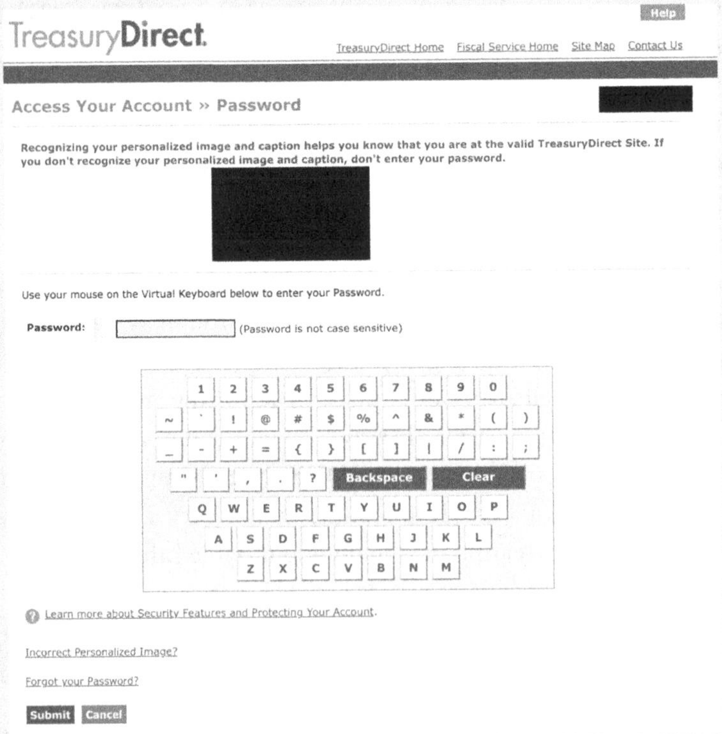

Figure 5.1   Login page of TreasuryDirect.

Remember that Starbucks example? Even if this is somehow implemented securely—I have no interest in testing it out without being invited formally by the Treasury to do so, on account of disliking orange-tinted overalls—the impact on the user in terms of nudging them towards picking a simple password is massive.

And remember, those passwords are not case sensitive; they won't be hard to crack.

Clearly, picking the right audits is a task that will often fall to the CISO (or their compliance manager). But that's obvious, and our goal here is to avoid being obvious.

In that spirit, here is where it gets really tricky. There are two contexts to consider, but they are really just two sides of the same coin:

As a customer (company, enterprise, agency, and so on), how do you evaluate your vendors' security posture and their audit range, scope, and quality?

As a vendor, how do you pick a set of audits and standards such that you end up demonstrating your security posture and projecting the right message to your target audiences in the most effective way possible?

In both cases, the security leader can be incredibly helpful—and harmful.

On the company/customer side, a too-rigid CISO that sees threats everywhere or is otherwise disengaged from the business can get sucked into the trap of being overly conservative. In such an environment, inevitably a checkbox mentality will eventually replace an actual security focus. Business leaders across the organization, under pressure to respond to the markets they operate in and the constituents they serve, will ultimately find ways to satisfy the burden of an ever-growing list of requirements, and they will do so by (1) rejecting many opportunities to utilize and implement technology enhancements, thereby putting their companies at a competitive disadvantage; or more likely, (2) by finding ways to circumvent overly burdensome requirements, trusting that things will go well in the end. In either case, they will report that everything is A-OK.

After all, things do usually go well. And even when they don't, it will be the CISO's fault.

Right?

And yes, that last bit is a true statement. Any security leader that creates so many obstacles in front of the business, even as they claim to serve the business, is at fault when it all comes crashing down. Excuses like "but they didn't follow my instructions!" will sound, and are, immature.

It is in these environments where audit reports become a means unto themselves, a way to mark checkboxes and no more. Sure, it satisfies the red tape. But it does nothing for the security posture of the organization whatsoever.

Not surprisingly, these happen to be the same organizations that allow their entire security program to be driven by compliance standards, to the exclusion of everything else. This model is known as "security by compliance," and you don't want it.

In one stereotypical example, we came in to advise a multi-billion-dollar multinational and at some point ran into one of those internal contradictions that is a classic sign of this particular malady. In this company's case, the issue quickly became starkly visible in change management.

They had, frankly, one of the best change management systems we'd ever seen. Everything was tracked, multiple approval chains were possible depending on criticality and urgency, with fallbacks and rollbacks built into the flows so that nothing falls through . . . it was, in every respect, an auditor's dream. We were duly impressed.

So . . . what's the problem?

Well, after being suitably blown away by how well changes were managed, we were faced with the challenge of somehow reconciling that with another piece of information we had already discovered. The company's overall rollback ratio—the number of changes that failed and had to be rolled back—was hovering around 15%.

One in six!

That, if you're not in technical operations, is a frighteningly large number. It is highly disruptive at such a level, especially when you're running a massive-scale platform like these guys were. Not only that, but this rate of failure had become the default expectation. Everywhere you looked, people accounted for this. It eats up resources like nobody's business to nurse along such an inherently unstable environment, because you constantly have to be on watch for the next failing change or series of changes and be able to react incredibly quickly while still striving to keep high reliability for the customers.

Forget four or five sixes. Can you make two? (two nines, or 99% uptime)

In other words, it's a nightmare.

Clearly, something wasn't working. A solid change management program is intended precisely to stop this sort of chaos. That's the reason to want to manage changes in the first place. Theirs was looking so nice and spiffy.

What gives?

Digging a little deeper, the answer quickly came into view. The number of changes they were approving, on a daily basis, was so large that it was manifestly impossible that they were all actually being reviewed. When we started interviewing the various change managers, we were easily able to confirm the truth: the volume (or velocity) of change was so high that they all independently came to the same (and only) practical solution. They simply approved every change without actually reviewing it.

In other words, it became . . . a process in checkboxing.

The change management system recorded these approvals appropriately, audit trails were generated, and everyone, especially the auditors, was happy. On paper, it all looked good. In reality, if it wasn't for incredibly strong tech-ops leaders that created a number of backstops to catch and handle failures once things crossed into their domain (production), it is entirely likely that business would have simply ground to a halt because of repeated technology failures. As it were, they had odd scalability issues even though they were at the bleeding edge of virtualization, and it was starting to hinder business growth.

I would suggest that this is not a desirable business outcome, change management be damned.

Needless to say, it is incredibly easy to point the fingers at tech-ops for this problem, because the underlying issue only becomes obvious in production (where the failures happen). In a big and fast-growing platform play, these kinds of business issues can result in billions of dollars of lost shareholder value.

Billions!

And the right person to identify them is not the CIO, or the CTO, or the COO, but rather the CISO. Grasping the dangerous impact of a seemingly successful yet ultimately failing change management process is part of their charter. There are plenty of other areas where this is true.

Let's now switch to the *vendor side*. Here, you tend to see a similar problem, only in reverse. The overly conservative (or, strangely, inexperienced) approach will result in a top-down "dictation methodology," where audits replace security as a measure of success. Assuming the company isn't slowed down dramatically as it attempts to handle all these audits in some operationally rational fashion—a big assumption—then surely it will make sales happy.

The problem arises when actual security problems are left unaddressed because the only measure of success is passing those audits. Real security issues don't necessarily crop up during an audit. Rather, the truth is that it is always possible to pass an audit if you want to, even if your house is on the proverbial fire. Gaming the process is pretty easy. The sadder truth is that security auditors are rarely if ever incentivized to challenge their clients' statements beyond a cursory level. If you look at the evolution of financial audits over the decades, you will see the exact same pattern repeating in the world of security audits right now. We're at that early stage where the collusion between client and auditor is almost inevitable, because the regulatory framework is mostly non-existent, and the risk–reward ratio is far too low to, uh, inspire confidence.

Put another way, if you can get away with it, what shouldn't you?

How do you think all these big breaches you hear about in the news happen when the companies are all supposedly compliant with their governing standards? Remember Target? They were "PCI compliant" when they got hit. How about TJ Max? Same story. Royal Bank of Scotland? You guessed it.

So the vendor adopts a security by compliance mentality, hires a friendly auditor, gets through as many things as they can imagine spending only what they have to in order to satisfy the audit process, and lets the rest take care of itself.

A few years back, in one of the sessions that VISA puts for PCI assessors (QSAs), they held up the PCI audit for Amazon AWS as an example. Yes, that one. You know why they presented it? As a lesson to QSAs on *how not to conduct a PCI audit*.

Now, don't get me wrong. Amazon's security posture is plenty strong. It has to be, in their case. They have no choice because they present one of the most appetizing targets for hackers anywhere. I have no reason to doubt that they do a good job over there. Their results speak for themselves, and incidentally, show how far-removed *actual* security is from security *compliance*.

But let me ask you: if Amazon "got away with it" in terms of one of their highly visible audits, how much confidence should you have in the multitude of much smaller vendors out there presenting a series of audit statements and reports? From a commercial perspective, by all means, accept the audits and move on, since it's the pragmatic approach. The contractual liability is what matters in the end, anyway. Just don't let it fool you into a false sense of, well, security.

What all this leads to is this. *Compliance should never, ever drive the security program. Instead, compliance should be a derivative of the security program.* A side benefit. A happy happenstance. It's really that simple. A well-designed security program will result in compliance audits becoming a "thing that happens" when the business needs it to happen, rather than something that dominates security efforts throughout the year and especially during audit times.

I was reminded of this in the last conference call we had leading into one of our clients' big audits, about a year into us working with them. They used to go through the annual "compliance time" process, where suddenly everybody remembers to do all the things they were supposed to, they all scramble to get it done and produce the minimum amount of necessary flimsy evidence, construct stories of plausible deniability, and otherwise pray it isn't too painful.

Compliance was always a fire. They expected it. They hated it.

The call took less than 20 minutes, out of a scheduled 2 hours. We reached the end of the list of items, and an uncomfortable silence erupted on the line. I counted to three and coughed. Then I addressed the compliance manager.

"So . . . let me guess. This seems too easy, right?"

He laughed nervously, joined by a couple of others.

"Feels like we're missing something, right? There isn't any fire? There has to be a fire," I admit, I was enjoying the moment. Maybe a bit too much.

He laughed again, then said "yeah, I'm not used to this. Last year at this time we were running all over the place, and I was trying to figure out if I would have a job when it was all done. I have this uneasy feeling at the pit of my stomach that we're forgetting something critical."

"We're not," I assured him. "It's just that security is working in a way that makes compliance a side-effect. That's all."

And that is how compliance should always be handled. I'll repeat the statement I made earlier, because I sometimes feel like I should create etched wooden plaques bearing it and hand them off to all our clients: *compliance just happens*. It's a side-effect of a good security program. Do you need to occasionally design and implement specific controls for compliance? Certainly. But if your entire budgeting process for security is justified by compliance mandates, then you're doing something wrong. Very wrong.

I trust that you see, as well, how a technical, conservative, severe, doom-and-gloom CISO ends up hurting themselves and the business they are hired to serve. In the end, if a breach happens, that CISO will lose their job anyway, because part of their job is to be the one that loses their job when something bad happens.

Go ahead, read that again.

They will not have protected the company; in fact, they will have weakened its overall security posture by insisting on the compliance process until it became the end goal, with predictable results.

A business-oriented CISO, on the other hand, will tend to partner more closely with other business leaders in the company, and find ways to support new business initiatives while considering and mitigating actual risks they might introduce. When trust is established through these channels, some of this will happen without direct involvement of the particular business leader or third party via "invisible technologies," as we discuss in the next chapter. They will understand how to navigate the world of security standards and how to interpret an audit report as it pertains to a vendor's proposed products and services. They will have a good grasp of liability and be able to guide security efforts while cracking a joke or two (imagine that).

And what about compliance?

I'm glad you asked.

Why, it will take care of itself.

I would like to share a guest essay from Steve Levinson, a dear friend and colleague who has managed to establish such a dedicated following of customers across so many industries that he might rightly be called a security compliance yogi:

VIEW FROM THE TRENCHES

TOO MUCH OF EVERYTHING IS JUST ENOUGH (STEVE LEVINSON)

One universal question that CISOs must be prepared to answer is *how much is enough security?* Somewhere on the continuum of possibilities between "you are so exposed that your pants are down to your ankles" and "we're perfectly secure" (which is a complete fallacy and should therefore be a cause for serious concern) is the level of security that aligns with your organization's risk appetite. A mantra that we often share with our clients is that "business always trumps security," but that it is critical to do business in a *reasonably secure* manner. What does this mean, and what factors should be considered? At a high level, you should consider the following:

- How sensitive is the data in our ecosystems? Do we have any particularly sensitive personally identifiable information such as social security numbers, payment card data, or electronic personal health information? Do we have any intellectual property stored electronically that we need to protect?

- What is the perceived value of the data in our ecosystems? What value is it to attackers? What value is it to our competitors, or in some cases foreign nation states?
- What industry regulations or laws must we abide by and what is expected in our vertical?
- What do our customers and partners expect from us? Remember that even if we think that the data is not sensitive, if our client or partner thinks it's sensitive, then by all means the data is sensitive!
- What is the potential for damage to our brand if we were breached?

As you can see, there are a myriad of levers to pull to try to figure out the right amount of security for your organization. Just as it would appear to be imprudent to spend $1,000,000 to protect $5 worth of data, it would also be imprudent to spend $5 to protect $1,000,000-worth of data. Compound this with the fact that some of these measures are subjective—you can't really place an exact value on your data, but you can usually at least get a sense within an order of magnitude of its value.

THE JURY IS OUT

Let's face it. There are no silver bullets. There are no solid formulas that tell you exactly what you must do to right-size security. A good CISO is like a Jedi knight—you must use common sense and intuition, combined with a well-thought-out strategy to help charter your course through the risk-infested waters. May the force be with you. Oftentimes, we tell our clients, "if you were to find yourself in front of a jury trying to explain your strategy as it pertained to *something that happened*, do you have a solid leg to stand on?" Similar to having to "prove your work" in math class, you should be able to prove to any jury that your approach to addressing risk has been thought out in a thorough and pragmatic manner.

Oh, and by the way, it is no longer even remotely acceptable to claim blissful ignorance as a defense. Once a vulnerability is publicly known, or once we know how that breached company from the headlines was compromised, it is incumbent upon us to proactively address that particular threat vector or risk. At this point, there's nowhere to hide, and you must exercise reasonable care to address this risk.

A well-thought-out security program is the underlying foundation that allows an organization to align risk management with business objectives. It is about the journey, not the destination, but you may as well enjoy the ride, or at least minimize the pain associated with it. The more you can infuse the right amount of security into your everyday business-as-usual processes, the less painful security will be.

AND SPEAKING OF WHICH ... HOW MUCH IS THE RIGHT AMOUNT OF COMPLIANCE?

First and foremost, compliance is a favorable byproduct of a good security program. If you lead with a robust and pragmatic security program, compliance will follow. Any CISO who builds their security program by trying to check the boxes to be compliant is just doomed for failure. The compliance framework(s) that best align for your business should generally be guidelines toward molding your Information Security program since they will ultimately be used to measure the success of your program. The degree to which you must demonstrate your compliance will vary, based on the aforementioned factors (sensitivity of data, industry, and what your customers and partners expect) combined with the perceived risk: can you impact the well-being of a *lot* of sensitive data or just a little bit? In what ways do you handle the data? What do you do with the data?

Invariably, you will need to demonstrate to someone (client, partner, regulator, or auditor) that you have established a sustainable program that adheres to whatever framework(s) best align either with your business vertical or with customer and partner perception and needs. The burden of proof will vary depending on the compliance framework selected to measure your security posture, from a short refreshing self-assessment questionnaire to a meticulously detailed on-site audit. Your security program should include controls that would create outputs that would provide necessary evidence, if called upon, to address the framework in question. Ideally, you will be making the smart spend on security (i.e., spending the "right" amount of time and money on your security program) as to right-size security while minimizing your spend on compliance to that which is necessary to demonstrate that you've exercised proper due diligence in adhering to the particular flavor-of-the-day compliance framework. A common mantra across the Information Security universe is that compliance does not equal security. This is not to say that you should skimp on your compliance efforts by either fudging your answers or by finding a check-the-box assessor who isn't really measuring your compliance. Rather, it is about trying to minimize this effort and spend to that which makes business sense.

5.2

VOLUNTARY
SELF-IMMOLATION

Since this book was first published, the voluntary compliance industry has exploded, pretty much as one expected it might. As we discussed, audit reports like SOC2 are very valuable within the sales process, and in recognition of this, many b2b organizations have chosen to pursue them with vigor. But with all good things come some bad, and the field of security is notorious for delivering undesirable outcomes (ha).

Let's address some of them.

First, a "fill-the-gaps" primer: *voluntary compliance* refers to that last category of security-related audits, at this time most commonly represented by two specific standards. One is SOC2, and the other is ISO27001. The latter has a number of offshoots that deal with privacy (like ISO27018 and ISO27701), and in itself incorporates a collection of standards within the ISO27000 series, but we deal with the larger picture in this book, so no more about that. The one thing I do want to make clear is that, contrary to what many practitioners will tell you for reasons that have more to do with egos than with reality, none of these are "easy" to attain and maintain.

The reason these audits are voluntary is that there is no regulatory, legal, or rules-based driver for adopting these standards, let alone getting audited against them. Keep that in mind; the word *compliance* is, perhaps, the greatest offender here, because it implies something (namely that there is some force of rule, law, or regulation driving these audits) that simply isn't true.

Which leads us to the obvious question: why on earth would a company subject itself to the often frustrating, onerous, and disruptive process of complying with something like this?

No, really. I want you to stop reading and take a moment to think through this.

DOI: 10.1201/9781003302759-11

Why?

Why do it at all?

And for extra points . . . why do it the way it's being done now?

Make sure you have your answer ready before we continue, because this is an area where the industry has not only led us astray but is also sledgehammering (is this a verb? It should be a verb) everyone with pointless and ultimately dangerous advice with the sole desire to feed itself.

Let's review the wrong answer first. It goes like this:

Q: Why should we pursue voluntary compliance?

A: Because these standards improve security within the organization.

When people say this, they are (I'm being kind) stretching these standards into the realm of being frameworks. Those, in turn, are another way in which self-important people who are *clearly* way smarter than you let you know that *you* don't know shit about nothing, but *they* do, and that's why you need to give them more money to do all the smart stuff.

Yes, you can use these standards, like you can any other standard (the NIST 800 series comes to mind), as a useful guide towards designing a reasonable security control matrix in any environment. As I mentioned elsewhere in this book, I regularly recommend that companies adopt the technical operations control set embedded in the PCI standard as a good way to protect whatever they deem to be sensitive data of any kind; PCI is an excellent technical data protection standard *independent of compliance*, precisely because it is so prescriptive, and there is no reason to limit its usefulness to credit cards. It's easy to understand and implement, too, which serves as a massive force multiplier.

But that's not what these people mean. Oh no. See, SOC2 is not very prescriptive, and is *completely compliance driven*, requiring an auditor to make judgment calls with respect to every singular element. As for ISO27001, that one's a *governance* standard, which means it's high-level, as far from boots-on-the-ground as you can imagine. It's a good way to think about how to manage a decent security program. The problem is that ISO27001, like all ISO standards, is an **extremely** persnickety, uncompromising, dense academic paper that ignores reality on the ground and deems itself as holy writ. A quick example: good luck arguing with your auditor that your security policies don't need a *specific* way of versioning incorporated into the documents themselves, even if that makes the documents more difficult to consume by their intended audience.

I mean, who cares about the *friendliness* of such documents? Since when has *approachability* been part of security? Right?

Right?

Formality rules!

What ends up happening in reality is that, if you take this approach, you end up spending a lot of money while pissing everybody off and making tons of compromises anyway in service of the business, and get so consumed with chasing your own tail that you forget (or ignore) everything that isn't directly tied to these standards. That does not a good security program make, but it does let you hire a lot of GRC analysts.

In the end, by buying into the idea that these standards should drive security, you are switching into a "security by compliance" mode. This is because humans are, well, human, and we will always default to easy mode when we can. SOC2 and ISO27001 naturally lend themselves to metrics, which are easily reportable, which we end up using … with the corollary being that we stop doing anything else.

So what's the right answer?

It's actually really simple, even downright obvious.

Let's roll back to the original driver for why we chose to voluntarily comply with anything in the first place, even though there is no rule forcing us to do so:

Because our customers feel the need for reassurance.

You're doing it because it helps your sales team. It enables them to sell more easily and more quickly to larger accounts in more geographic regions (ISO27001, being what it is, has a much larger impact for non-US sales).

So as much as the following statement regularly pisses off everyone involved in the massive, remarkably complicated and cumbersome apparatus of both SOC2 and ISO27001 (and whichever one becomes big next; I think people are salivating about an auditing standard for the NIST-800 series), it does still benefit from being factual:

These audit reports are sales tools.

That's it.

They have no other legitimate purpose.

I strongly suggest that we stop pretending otherwise.

While you can use them to your advantage in other ways, like informing your security program, that's a side-effect, not a *purpose*. And yes, the distinction is critical, because the moment you stop pretending is the moment you can go back to managing said security program, rather than some twisted two (or more) headed compliance hydra.

This leads us to another painful example of how the security industry has really taken it to the nth degree, and made life miserable for everybody: compliance automation tools.

Yes, I'm looking at you, Vanta, and your industry peers (e.g. Drata, SecureFrame, Tugboat, and so on; this stuff changes so quickly that the names don't matter).

Here is the theoretical value proposition for these tools: buy me, and I'll make your process of complying with SOC2 (let's go with that one) easier.

And how would that come to be?

Because the tool would grab all the niggly bits of evidence from all across the entire environment, and sort it out automagically for auditor examination. You, the customer, don't need to do anything! It just happens!

We're pretty deep into this book, so you already know I'm all about hidden assumptions, because that's how you get bit in the royal patootie. There is a brobdingnagian one buried in here.

Can you spot it?

Before I state the answer, let me add that these vendors—some of them more than others, with a particularly offensive one doing so acutely—pretty much suggest that you just give your SOC2 auditor direct access to the tool to see things for themselves. That one vendor will even happily help you select an auditor from a list, and . . . *cough* . . . tell you that if you work with their tool and an auditor from their list, you'll have a super easy time with it.

Anyway.

So what's the problem here?

Well, if you've ever run a security program in a high-growth technology organization—the vast majority of customers for these tools—then you know that your environment is in constant flux. You also know that new things show up overnight all the time, and that to stay sane, you have to take a pragmatic approach, letting some things go, and focusing on what's important. First and foremost, that would be customer data systems, because that's where the liability is, and that focus happens to naturally and happily align with business goals.

Or at least, that's how you *should* be running your program. So many don't, which is why I wrote this book in the first place.

So now comes your compliance management tool, and hooks into everything, and collects everything all the time like the soulless machine that it is, and then at audit time, hands it over to the auditor.

So what happens next?

The obvious: the auditor, who *doesn't, cannot,* and *never will* have the context necessary to actually understand your environment and its internal risks, is presented with a myriad of exceptions, issues, and problems that they must now address in the audit. At that point, it really doesn't matter how much explaining you are willing to do—you're gonna have to fix things so that the tool is happy so that the auditor is happy. Even if the vast majority of the tool's "findings" are irrelevant, stale, out of what you would consider proper scope, or downright stupid.

The tool doesn't know.

The auditor has no context (and often neither knowledge nor experience in security), but they have a reporting tool.

And your security program inevitably aligns itself to serve the almighty compliance software god, because sales needs the sales tool (a.k.a. audit report) and that's how you produce it for them.

Worse, because you've never understood how these audits actually work, you can't even begin to do the explaining, and you have no choice, because all the problems I described earlier keep increasing at a furious pace—new features, new systems, and a rapidly changing landscape.

All those engineers you hired have to keep developing your products, after all.

So now you get into the trap that the tool maker set for you all along. Following that "easy" first year, by the time year two rolls around, you're a captive audience. You're locked in. You can't extricate yourself from the compliance valley of darkness, not even if you realize what's going on and try to change it; good luck justifying an even greater expense than you were trying to eliminate in the first place by buying the tool in order to replace it with, you know, an actual program.

Of course the solution to this is obvious: never, *ever* allow an auditor in the voluntary compliance realm anywhere near your actual evidence repo. At least not before you curate it so that it at least represents the security reality on the ground in your environment.

And therein lies the hidden assumption: that by having the auditor "see" everything, one gets a higher quality audit. That somehow, accuracy matters. Of course it doesn't; you hired them, and the SOC2 auditors don't want you to present a challenging situation; it's less profitable for them. And they most certainly won't fail you if they have any possible way to avoid that; they want your repeat business.

Remember, this is all *voluntary*.

That's why all these audits always have a lengthy period of, err, exception negotiations. Isn't it better to avoid them in the first place by, well, knowing what you're doing?

And no, folks, this isn't lying. It's *application of context*, which is exactly the entire purpose for one's existence as a security leader (remember that little thing about "managing risk"?). And to do this correctly, you need someone who understands how the audits themselves are structured. Not a soulless machine whose purpose is to enrich both its software maker and, to a lesser degree, their auditing partners.

Interestingly enough, such a person will usually end up buying one of these tools just to help themselves in getting certain types of evidence flowing to their internal repo. But they would be managing the tool and handling the audit, and their expertise will make the outcome a lot more predictable and a lot less painful for everyone involved.

Note that this also removes vendor lock-in—if you have someone who knows what they are doing on top of things, then you are no longer dependent on a particular piece of automation that works really hard to ensure you can't easily switch to something else. That alone tells you everything you need to know about these compliance tools.

So does this mean that SOC2 audit reports, ISO27001 certifications, and the rest are worthless?

Of course not. I think they are extremely useful and valuable, as long as they are kept in the proper context—as sales tools.

And why should the enterprise customer trust them?

Because of two reasons.

One is that contrary to what the holier-than-thou crowd will tell you, getting through these audits does require a fair bit of work, no matter how you approach it. So yes, a SOC2 audit report does evidence at least a common level of security controls in an environment. It may not be totally accurate, but it's good enough to tick the box, and that's a whole lot more than nothing. Plus accuracy is a dumb concept when one acknowledges the reality that all of it changes on an hourly basis.

The second reason is even simpler, as we have previously discussed: liability. What voluntary compliance audits achieve is the commercial miracle of allowing two parties to agree on a common, industry-standard way in which the vendor can satisfy the customer about an area that would otherwise require tremendous complexity to handle.

And if any of you think that you can do a better job than your vendor's invited voluntary compliance auditor, who does this all day every day, in auditing the vendor's security apparatus . . . all I have to say to you is that you're no more than an empire-builder who wants to "run a large team."

Or you're delusional.

Take your pick.

So what should we do, Barak? As the enterprise customer in this equation, do we trust these audits or don't we?

The answer is you do and you don't. You do insofar as the contract goes. You also remember that you can't manage your security program to compliance standards, and you make sure that you control tightly the data sets you share with each vendor. Working as CISO for SaaS and PaaS vendors I've heard, too many times, a version of the following statement from enterprise customers:

"We can't trust our own teams to manage their data properly."

This was provided as an excuse as to why they employ an incredibly and unnecessarily cumbersome vendor risk management process that their internal business owners hate with a passion. My answer has always been… "then regardless of what I tell or show you, why should you trust mine?"

No, I haven't lost a sale ever because of that answer.

And that also, neatly, reinforces the reality of voluntary compliance: the only companies who choose to undergo these audits are, by and large, those SaaS and PaaS vendors. You won't usually find them in b2c organizations, and not because their security programs are worse. It's because the b2b folks need to sell, and that's an established way to reduce sales friction.

Like we said . . . sales tools.

Switching back to the enterprise, let me then offer a really simple way to manage your third-party (usually cloud these days) vendors that is effective and will give you the same level of protection as any convoluted process might in any way that actually matters.

Note that this ignores *mandated compliance* audits (like PCI). For example, if you share credit card numbers with your vendor, then they have to be PCI compliant.

To begin, each vendor is initially classified as one of three tiers, at the highest level which matches the description:

High—vendor has external (usually remote) access to our own environment (tiny number, often zero)
Medium—vendor handles our and/or our customers' sensitive data
Low—everybody else (this should be at least 50% of the total)

All vendors in the medium or high category are *required* to provide some form of voluntary compliance audit report and maintain them throughout the contract.

Vendors in the medium category who handle our *customers'* data (usually PII) must sign a data protection addendum.

Vendors in the "low" category are asked for any audit reports, and those who can provide them are evaluated internally as less risky and more desirable; in other words, in choosing between two vendors, one of which can provide a report and one which cannot, we lean towards the former. We wish to reward them for thinking about security and giving us reassurances, don't we?

Vendors in the high category must agree that, while they work in our environment, they must abide by our security policies at all times, just like contractors do.

And our data security addendum is then shortened to capturing the commitment to provide these audit reports on a regular cadence, plus a couple of other key provisions: data retention, incident response, and enforcement of the same rules on their downstream providers that are involved with delivering services to us.

That's it.

You're done.

It may feel scary, but guess what? All you're giving up is the *illusion* of control you never really had. You can't manage your vendors' security programs, but let's admit it, as an enterprise customer, you can (and often do) bully them in the contract anyway. So let's put our big girl panties on, shall we? In return, we gain significant efficiencies in our internal sourcing operations, and even more importantly, a much happier bunch of internal colleagues and business partners, who are subsequently much more likely to be receptive to our security pleas in areas that actually matter.

That's an equation everybody should appreciate.

6

TECHS-MECHS

Yes, the title is word play on the term "Tex-Mex," only with technologies and mercenaries. Did I just explain my own joke? Talk about failing! Moving on …

Having spent this book convincing you that information security should be considered a matter of everything besides technology …

I think it's time to talk about technology.

Because even though technology is not what security is about, as we can now hopefully all agree, the discipline is still grounded in the proper use of, and risks of using, technology. After all, Chief Security Officers of prior eras often concerned themselves with keeping things safe in physical safes. Today's CISOs can rarely even tell the difference between time and area resistance ratings.

"You're doing what?!"

My colleague's stunned tone speaks for itself. The gentleman we are speaking to, a senior software architect, happily repeats his last statement, seemingly beaming with pride.

"Yeah, we've implemented our own stack. It works faster this way, and it's just as secure."

This would not be the first time we had heard this sort of claim, in a number of different technical realms. But it does stand out this time, because the particular area of discussion is encryption key management, and in particular, key generation.

A short conversation ensues and we learn that the company didn't like how slow AES was, so they took it upon themselves to develop their own implementation (or "stack," apparently) of AES-128.

DOI: 10.1201/9781003302759-12

Note that this implementation was the critical component protecting the company's core technology. If it got broken, it would be a potentially catastrophic event. They would likely lose 90% of their client base in a few weeks.

That's what they told us, anyway.

This "custom implementation" coded into their proprietary platform was based on SSL with a couple of shortcuts (including changing from the default 10 rounds to 6 and using a semi-fixed initialization vector tied to minor software revisions—things we could tell sounded strange without having a degree in crypto) and, well, it sure was astonishingly fast.

Amusingly, the BEAST attack was made public just weeks before.

Sadly, the company insisted that what they were doing was perfectly safe, and as proof, provided the resume of the guy who designed it. He had a PhD in Computer Science and studied crypto so, we were told, he knew what he was doing.

Plus he wasn't working there anymore and they were too afraid to mess with it.

The kind of attitude in the story above is more prevalent than anyone might care to admit, especially in technology-oriented disciplines. We often tend to defer to the authority of those who can present impressive educational credentials, and for their part, many folks with such credentials do not hesitate to use them as a cudgel.

It's easier that way.

The term "hacker" doesn't necessarily mean "person who wishes to do you harm." It also means "someone who likes to tweak technology."

Ironically, in security implementations, this attitude can be devastating.

But first, let us (again) reframe our conversation. For that, I'd like to ask another question:

Who ends up in security, anyway?

I don't mean the kind of folks who are the modern version of those who discovered their life calling in Web design in the late Nineties. Jumping on the bandwagon is all well and good, and essential once a bandwagon is there to jump on. I can say with conviction that a career in security really is a terrific idea, and I highly recommend it. Security is now and will continue to be a growth industry for a while to come.

Rather, I am referring to the people who end up in security because it makes a sort of twisted sense to them, for whom it is the field that they gravitate toward naturally. The combination of an asymmetric playing field (and one in which the attacker—that is, the other side—has a built-in advantage), a highly stressful environment, an almost structural and practically guaranteed lack of appreciation, and a strong likelihood to be considered "at fault" when something goes wrong . . . put these things together and you've got to wonder who, in their right mind, would want to pick security as a career.

And yet, those of us who end up here . . . we choose it anyway.

Why? Why willingly subject ourselves to this madness, when we could so easily do well in more established technology-related areas, like coding or networking?

And who are we?

A deep interest in technology is indeed a common theme, as one might expect.

It is less in the building of things, which leads to successful careers in fields like software and hardware design, and more in breaking things apart to see how they really work—and then improving them. I doubt that there is a single security-minded professional out there who does not have a childhood story about taking something apart out of curiosity, then putting it back together, often in unintended clever ways that give it additional function. I did it myself, with more things than I can count. It led to my first small business, of building custom gaming PCs, which I started out doing out of love for tinkering, and later on for a few others who were impressed by the results. In hindsight, I was running this little business illegally—I imported custom components from the United States by asking anybody I knew who went there to buy them for me and bring them back, thereby avoiding hefty import taxes. This practice provided me with a small sales margin that was just enough to buy components for my own rig, seeing as I never charged for labor. But the truth is, I never thought of it as a business, rather as sharing my love of computing and gaming with my friends/clients, and that mindset of figuring things out for the love of tinkering truly seems like a defining theme in the ranks of security people.

A strong technology background is therefore essential for a good security leader. Ironically, that is the fix we often find ourselves in, the crux of the conundrum if you will. It is so easy for someone so steeped in technology to turn to technology as the solution to problems that they understand so well. Yet, as we have previously discussed, security is as much about people as it is about machines, and a security leader lacking a thorough understanding of people's behavioral patterns is one that is walking around deaf and blind.

Although certainly not mute.

Until about a decade ago, the most common technology background for security leaders was in networking and routing, often with a strong technical operations focus. Understanding data and traffic flows in a complex networked environment is still an important technical background for the seasoned security leader, just as a background in law enforcement was essential for the physical security-focused leader of yesteryear, and a background in application security is now the key ingredient for the modern CISO who is tasked with risk management in a virtualized cloud environment.

A network-focused background leads to a network-oriented solution matrix. Because so much of the security product space originates from this area, this is also where most common language is available, where solutions are most mature, and where budgets are easiest to obtain. Even the least technical executive—say, a marketing chief with no technology background—has at least a vague notion that a firewall is important and that it protects the network in some essential fashion. In fact, arguably, the first network security product to make it big in this modern technology world was Checkpoint's Firewall-1 (with my sincerest apologies to anti-virus makers).

It made sense too. In the old days, companies and other connected entities had fully controlled, internal networks, with a very clear demarcation point between themselves and the rest of the world at the Internet connection (in those days, often only one). It made perfect sense for one to protect that point first—if you could stop the "bad people" from coming through there, then you wouldn't have to worry about what's on the inside. A bit like that guard standing in the front gate of the proverbial castle. As long as you defended the gate well,

Figure 6.1   Cisco advertisement, asking people if it makes sense to protect their house with doors from so many manufacturers.

your people will live a happy, fulfilling life in your main courtyard. In fact, that image has such lasting power over our imaginations, and is so pervasive and irresistible, that Cisco—a technology behemoth with a massive security product portfolio—came out in February 2017 with an evocative image to represent its security product line (Figure 6.1). Do you see the implied message? To protect your house—your castle—you need to make sure nobody bad comes through the door.

This line of thinking is still extremely prevalent today, with the primary fear in security being of hackers coming in from the outside. No wonder so many people are still stuck in the "let's build a big wall" mindset. It doesn't matter that most experts and independent research point to insider threat as the primary cyber risk factor for organizations. We *know* the people on the inside. They can't *possibly* be any scarier than those malicious, faceless hackers from Russia or China.

This sort of protection, called perimeter defense, is still a crucial part of any security strategy, but the world has evolved dramatically in the past 20 years. The number of connections to the outside world—to third-party partners, customers, vendors, and even competitors—seems to grow exponentially with every passing day. That's even before you consider the impact of a public cloud environment, where a company no longer even controls the underlying assets—the servers and network—over which their data is stored and transmitted. A common network today no longer has clear boundaries.

Oh, and each of these connection points, called an API (Application Programming Interface), uses its own custom language, and while companies are slowly but increasingly trying to protect the externally facing APIs . . . internal APIs are usually wide open to anyone with established user credentials. Which can lead to all sorts of fun situations, as illustrated in the next sub-chapter.

All of this comes before you even consider internal threats and the reality that practically any serious attack starts with compromising *people*, not machines.

In other words, there is no longer a "castle" (or home) to protect. To continue the analogy, you can think of the modern world of technology as fractional ownership gone mad.

The security world has been attempting to address this knowledge gap for many years using the "defense in depth" concept, originated by the NSA and popularized, to the best of my knowledge, by a luminary of the security world, Dr. Bruce Schneier. The idea behind defense in depth is that one has to erect multiple obstacles for compromising data, using a combination of different types of controls (physical, technical, and administrative) in different points within the chain.

But it's hard to argue against all these marketing dollars, and the end result is that it is still incredibly common to see organizations interpret "defense in depth" as multiple *technical* controls, and, more specifically, *network* controls. For example, internal segmentation (the separation of the internal network into multiple distinct zones) with a physical or virtual firewall at each internal connection point is often pointed to as evidence of a defense in depth approach.

That is wrong, and self-defeating, because it can instil a false sense of security, generally the most dangerous (and common) source of misplaced trust in security management.

Defense in depth is, in a simplified form, a way to delay an attacker from successfully compromising their target and exfiltrating (or stealing) the desired data, while at the same time alerting the defenders to the presence of the attack so that they can mitigate it before it ultimately succeeds. To do that, the security design must adopt different controls at different stages, with independent reporting mechanisms.

Let's examine how a properly segmented network with firewalls (or representations of them, such as security groups) at each choke point fails the defense in depth test.

As an attacker, I will likely attempt to first compromise and obtain legitimate user credentials—maybe by socially engineering an internal user of the network. These days, this is often accomplished by "Phishing," which involves tricking a user into disclosing their credentials to someone they believe they can trust. It could even be a user at a partner network that has little security in place, but legitimate access into the environment (the Target breach allegedly started by a compromise of a user account at their AC vendor).

Once I am inside the network with my newly acquired legitimate credentials, I'll focus on elevating my internal privileges to those of a user with access across the network. If security in this organization focuses on firewalls, network-based intrusion detection, and anti-malware, then it is likely that I will ultimately succeed without being noticed, as long as I conduct my authorized (remember that I have legitimate credentials) user activities stealthily. Now all those firewalls are useless; I don't have to break them, because I can traverse their boundaries legitimately using the compromised legitimate credentials. All that is left for me is to access my target system, obtain the desired dataset, and exfiltrate it—maybe by transitioning it back into the user network and hiding it inside of ordinary user access to the Web.

In fact, this description outlines a common footprint of many a successful breach (random recent big one: Twitter). The details change, but the overall approach does not. And there are so many ways to compromise a single user, especially in a large organization, that I regularly recommend to our customers at Eammune to consider and treat their user population as *compromised by definition*, assume that this population *can never be trusted*, and design their security controls with that assumption firmly in place.

In the world of technical security controls, this concept is called "Zero Trust." Unfortunately, like everything else in security, the marketers have already corrupted it beyond recognition.

Another example: one control that is found in every security standard is that of "one role per server." That makes sense. If you limit the function of a device to doing one thing, it is much easier to ensure that the device performs only that assigned role and no other.

But how do you carry this into the world of cloud? What does it even mean when you don't know what server group you're running on, let alone have access to the underlying operating system? Clearly, we have to evolve this idea into "one role per *service*," and change the entire way we view the functionality of our discreet platform components.

If you haven't heard of immutable containers yet, you will soon enough.

Well then, how do you deal with testing the security of those custom APIs? In the good ol' days of the Naughties, you could run a scanner against any Web application, and discover vulnerabilities because they all used a common protocol (HTTP) and functionally did the same thing (serve Web pages). An entire, multi-billion dollar testing industry was erected on this foundation.

Isn't that nice.

Because in today's world, while the underlying protocol (or rather, communications channel) may still be the same (ports 80 and 443) out of convenience, nothing that happens inside of it is standardized. Each application has its own, unique interface, and there is absolutely no master database of vulnerability signatures you can acquire that will allow you to test that interface.

Running standardized Web-app scans against custom APIs is mostly useless, but people do it all the time, and pat themselves on the back because they get back "clean" (or even "stealth mode") results. While it is true that common attack vectors are also not possible when every API has its own language, the ways in which one compromises software have not changed, and if someone wants to get you, all they have to do is read the API documentation and start coming up with clever ideas on how to mess with the published calls. You thought SQL injection was a big deal? How about SQL injections hidden inside of nontestable and effectively unmonitored API calls that get routed willy-nilly directly into the database, once authenticated?

This is the reality out there, and it's getting worse. Hackers have, if anything, an even easier time, because once they figure out how to communicate with the API, something that might be as complicated as reading publicly available instruction manuals, they have to worry a lot less about being caught in the act. Yes, there are API firewalls, but even today, few companies implement them.

So you run penetration tests? How good is the team you've hired? And more importantly, did you explain your API to them in detail? Or are they just doing a "blackbox" test, without prior knowledge? Because let me tell you something: the vast majority of pentesting out there is still focused on the network side, and even application pentests usually look for issues with common protocols.

Here is a question with an alarmingly low yes-to-no ratio: did you give them all your mobile apps (including your own testing ones with all the commands that are not part of the commercial release), so they could run it through a proxy (like Burp Suite) and try to break your API that way?

Your pentesters have access to the same tools that hackers do, but unless you pay them to manually figure out how to break your API, they won't even try.

They can't. They have nothing to go on. How many of these tests include both a "blackbox" component, and an "informed" component, do you think? The answer is, very few. And even if you did engage in thorough technical testing . . . what about the human element? Of the vast number of penetration tests performed annually, only very few actually include a social engineering component, which one might consider self-defeating seeing how many real-life breaches start by the compromise of an (innocent or not) human insider.

It is a sad reality that many companies prioritize surface tests or vulnerability scans, preferably with "clean" results, over a comprehensive test with the potential for discovering real issues. This is usually (and ironically) because of compliance mandates requiring "clean" results every 6 or 12 months, and it compounds the problem of having a false sense of security. All it does is serve to mask the existence of real problems—until the inevitable breach.

Worse, enterprise security departments who have forgotten their mission insist on "clean" pentests as a condition for signing a deal, further reinforcing the checkboxing nature of pentesting on the vendor side. They never stop to consider that solid, rigorous pentesting is likely to come up with something ugly, and that a company that gets these kinds of tests *regularly* also knows how to handle them *appropriately*. There is great nuance here, in being able to interpret these results not through the lens of severity rankings, but as part of an overall posture.

But we like checkboxes, and it's much easier to pretend we're reviewing security than admit we're just engaging in pointless CYA exercises. Plus let's be honest with ourselves, strong cyber talent isn't going to be interested in reviewing vendor pentests every day.

It's almost as if we prefer to stick our heads in the sand. And the compliance industry with its sharp focus on "passing" tests actively encourages this behavior!

Inspiring confidence, after all, is what we're all about.

Having covered our human tendency to have faith in our ability to skirt disaster even when skating while plastered, let us now turn to another serious yet common challenge. The security industry is chock-full of niche solutions—simply put, there is an incredibly high level of vendor and solution fragmentation. Sifting through them is difficult and requires experience in many fields. Obviously, if one's main expertise is in software, then one would feel most comfortable with application security solutions and tend to overlook the importance of other types of controls.

Putting that aside for the moment, the real obstacle here is in understanding the generally complex landscape of information security, and somehow emerging with a suite of solutions that would actually drive a benefit for the business without being wasted or worse, hamper productivity.

What do I mean by this?

Let's use a well-known example, which is the SIEM—Security Information and Event Monitoring tools. Generally speaking, these solutions attempt to collect security events across the many different discreet components in the environment, such as network and security devices, operating systems, and mission-critical applications. They then try to automate the process of sifting through these various alerts, correlating and analyzing them, so that in the end, the security operations team can get only the potentially meaningful indications of actual security events, to which they can respond effectively.

Conceptually, this category of solutions is highly valuable to any security operations teams. Indeed, it is impossible to consider a successful modern security operations shop that does not have some form of correlated event monitoring, alerting and response in place.

But the devil, as they say, is in the details. The first SIEMs quickly became notorious for being "expensive doorstops"—tools acquired and barely used. In many cases, they ended up fulfilling a role as a compliance checkbox, as in "yes auditor, we have event monitoring, just look at the pretty console." The reasons behind this are many, but the main ones are the following:

- SIEMs require a significant amount of investment in tuning and developing specific use-cases, otherwise they are far too noisy to manage. The unfortunate reality of security is that an incident will usually occur under the guise of being a legitimate event. Malicious parties often go to great lengths to hide their tracks, because effecting a breach is usually simply a matter of time, and the more time one can stay hidden while breaching, the better the chances are of stealing something important. In one case that speaks to the power and expense of running a SIEM effectively, a fortune-100 had an ongoing quarterly consulting expense item for $250,000 (in the Naughties!) to develop and implement one new use-case. Each and every Quarter. Most CISOs I know would salivate at such a budget opportunity. Most would also never get anywhere near it. Ransomware has only made things worse in the sense that it has dramatically shortened the life cycle of a breach; once you get it deployed, the monetization will occur *after* you've been discovered. It's a feature of this type of attack.

- SIEMs require constant TLC—in developing new use-cases, adjusting existing ones to the rapidly evolving technology infrastructure in a modern enterprise, and incorporating new types and kinds of alerts. Without such care, the SIEM configuration will rapidly go stale, and just as rapidly increase its noise-to-signal ratio. This creates a negative feedback loop, with mounting frustration on the part of the poor schmuck who is tasked with keeping the beast alive. And yet, it is impossible to do this without a business commitment across the board to continue to feed and care for the SIEM, even if only by informing the security operations center (SOC) of any and all changes in the environment, something that unfortunately rarely happens.

- The biggest enemy of security operation is . . . can you guess? Routine. When your job is to look at the exact same thing every day, and on the vast majority of days the thing looks exactly the same as it did the day before, then our brains tend to shortcut a little bit. Or maybe a lot. One of the purported advantages of a good SIEM is to avoid this problem—a machine doesn't get tired—but even so, an improperly maintained and configured SIEM will still generate a lot of unnecessary alerts, adopting the role of the boy who cried wolf, and eventually the brains of the humans operating the SIEM will tend to drift. The truth is that for most environments, real security incidents are few and far between, and people do usually move onwards with their careers leading to knowledge drain . . . all of this inevitably leads to many small cracks in the shell.

All it takes is one.

Another related problem is also driven by carbon life forms. Security people—at least those that gravitate to it naturally—are typically curious, creative, technologically inclined, and smart. Put someone like that in a position of handling routine, drab tasks, and they will quickly get bored and demoralized. The truth is that security operations teams can and do fail simply by hiring wrong. It's hard to find people with the talent and intelligence to properly interpret security events in real time, the discipline to continue to follow the response process day in and day out, and the fortitude to remain engaged. This particular skillset does point at something, though: folks with a military or law enforcement background may have certain built-in advantages in this particular area, and my own experience confirms this, at least empirically. My opinion is that it is much easier to train people, who already have self-discipline and demonstrated grit, in the realm of security operations, than it is to train your typically brilliant information security types into having self-discipline.

This one issue is so significant that an entire industry was created to address this problem—MSSPs (Managed Security Services Providers). These companies specialize in placing, configuring, managing, and most importantly, reacting to security events, so that their customers don't have to do so. Unfortunately, they tend to suffer from certain pervasive problems. First, they regularly oversell their services. For example, most systems and event logs don't necessarily benefit from real-time event monitoring and alerting, and to pretend otherwise creates alert fatigue. Fundamentally, there is nothing wrong with a less tiresome, daily or even weekly check of many of those feeds, but it is harder to organize and less profitable to sell that, so nobody does. Second, MSSPs can suffer from the same personnel issues as any company attempting to otherwise implement a SIEM, only on a larger scale.

Ultimately, any MSSP, by the very definition of their offered services, is "garbage in, garbage out." If you engage with them regularly, they will do you right. If you buy their service and then expect it to just work for you, then you will be disappointed. The MSSP doesn't have your local context; somebody has to respond to them regularly to make sure they can tweak their algorithms and responses to match your reality, just like you would have to do with your in-house SOC.

Still, and because of all the human challenges involved, I am generally a fan of outsourcing routine security operations tasks, if only because they often equal drudgery, and are rarely anywhere near the core competence of the business.

If you're not in the security operations business, then you don't have any business building your own SOC.

A related issue is that even a good SOC will fail (dramatically) if it does not have a true mandate to facilitate incident response. Unfortunately, this is another area where the human factor complicates things. The simple irritation factor that arises from business owners constantly being barraged by response requests from the SOC can create a culture where incident response is something that tends to be reflexively ignored. To recall an earlier story in this book, in one company I served, a highly accomplished CISO managed to only survive for only 10 months; he did that by making the mistake of believing that people cared to hear about all the problems. He created a highly visible incident response process, started showing his executive peers what was really going on . . . and ended up leaving when they pointed out that before he joined, the company never had so many security incidents.

Once you're done laughing, I'll point out that it's the CISO that failed here. It's the theme of this book, after all. This CISO should have understood the culture of the organization before embarking on this approach to "fixing" the security apparatus. The CISO ignored the culture, and the culture showed the CISO the door.

I would argue that human frailties are the biggest reason behind the vast majority of security failures, which conveniently leads us to the beginning of an answer to the question: how do we handle security technology acquisitions effectively?

To describe a class of solutions towards which I naturally gravitate, let me introduce a term I like to use in this context: *invisible technologies*.

What does this mean?

Ideally, an invisible technology is one that enforces a critical security policy without making the users of the technology aware of its existence. In other words, it is invisible to the typical end user. As a somewhat elaborate example, let's consider the area of access control. There are many ways to manage access—here are some of them:

- *By Segmentation*: Your "internal" pool of users are trusted, and all have access to the same shared resources. Once you're in, you're in. This approach is extremely prevalent. It also violates the principle of defense in depth and is otherwise a poor approach to controlling access to sensitive resources and data; one successful phishing attempt and everything goes up in smoke.

- *By Individual Access Profile*: Some users are given access to specific resources by virtue of authentication (say, logging in with a user and password combination). Other users may be able to reach the same resources (or "see them on the network") but will not be able to login to use them. There are a lot of challenges here, including the classic one where privileges are pretty much always added but never removed. Even when users switch jobs within the company, it is rare that anybody ever audits their access to see if it still is appropriate in their new role, and as a result, the longer a particular employee is with the company, the more extensive their overall access profile becomes. I call this SBAC, for "Seniority-Based Access Control."

- *By Role (Role-Based Access Control [RBAC])*: Each user's access profile is composed of a known role (or more likely, a series of roles), which is in turn based on their job description and duties. The combination of privileges associated with the different roles assigned to a user defines which resources that user may access. It is generally much easier to ensure users only have the access they need under the RBAC model, because as users change roles within the organization, all it takes is for someone to remove their prior role from their profile and add a new one instead, something that can be easily tied to, and automated via, the related HR action. RBAC is the method considered best practice in most security standards, although it does make a lot of unsafe assumptions about the people managing the RBAC system: that they would fully know how to configure it correctly, repeatedly, on a consistent basis, and never make mistakes.

- *By Data Classification*: Usually combined with RBAC, this approach handles the backend of role-based access, that is, determining in advance which classes of data are accessible by which role, and then classifying all data in the organization according to an established scheme. This is the most complicated approach, and while it sounds great in theory, it fails regularly in practice, as Wikileaks and countless others have shown. The reason is simple enough, as I am sure you have surmised by now. Humans have to manage this stuff, and humans are prone to failure, especially process failure, and especially as part of routine task management. There is also the matter of culture. Even the strictest of government agencies that may do well in training their staff on the importance of access management and protecting from data leaks rarely if ever do the same for all their contractors. Hello, Ed Snowden.

These and other ways are available to handle access to restricted data, including the use of different authentication methods, organizing resources, organizing the data on those resources, and so on. But in all cases, users are aware of two things: they can generally reach (or be aware of) systems that have data to which they should not have access, and there is data on those systems that they are not allowed to see. Both of these assumptions are fair, correct, and normal in a work environment.

Now let's add the human factor. The above has an obvious corollary in the form of a hidden assumption, which is this: any data available to a user is intended for them to see, *data classification policies be damned*.

Forget the policies for the moment, and focus on human behavior. Do you see how it all breaks apart?

In any access control scheme, you can trade complexity for security, but one way or another, you are dealing with people. Say you take the technically appropriate and more complex approach, combining RBAC with data classifications. Someone will inevitably forget to properly assign a label to some piece of data, or to remove a profile from a user account, and that user will suddenly represent a potential data leak, due to no fault of their own. They will naturally assume that they are supposed to see that data and share it, or maybe their account will become an entry point for someone else wanting access to such data, and any number of other attack vectors will open up. Now scale this up to a large organization, and those precious policies you forgot about are worth less than the paper they are written on.

An invisible technology implementation here will arrange things slightly differently. It will organize information in role-based vaults (matching RBAC and/or classification decisions) and then simply hide the existence of inappropriate ones from unauthorized roles. This may not sound so different, but notice the impact on human behavior. Users' assumptions are now different. They know there are systems they can't even see, and that they contain data to which they shouldn't have access. But we're used to that idea in our daily lives. Users will still tend to assume that data they can access are fair game, but because access is defined by vaults (like buildings in the real world), they would also be much more likely to notice (and report!) when unexpected access opens up for them to a new vault.

Psychologically, it works better for the humans.

It's a subtle difference, but one that can make all the difference. What it does require, though, is for network and data architects to make this a reality. By implication, it requires data owners to decide which vaults their data should go into, as opposed to forcing the organization to go through endless and failure-prone data classification exercises. But it also makes more sense; by designating vaults and letting data owners know where they can deposit data based on their understanding of its sensitivity, it places classification decisions where they should reside.

Combine that with a default "internal use only" approach that states that any data is by default available to everyone in the company unless otherwise designated by its owner, and you get a system that is far easier to handle, and, ultimately, far less susceptible to inadvertent leaks.

One last note with respect to classification. If you really feel that your data classification scheme deserves a matrix with 25 different choices (they exist out there), then you are too enamored of your process and completely removed from operational reality. Nobody can remember something like that unless it is their specific job to do so, and it gets annoying super-quick. Avoid classification fatigue. Simplify your classification scheme. Please.

Oh, and clearly, the addition of big data systems will shuffle the cards in this particular hypothetical, although not as much as you think.

If the last example was maybe a bit too complicated, consider a different one: firewalls and intrusion detection systems automatically block most bad traffic from coming through the network perimeter. It doesn't require any involvement or awareness from the typical user for this to happen. Firewalls are a wonderful example of a highly effective invisible technology and, I would argue, this is one of the big reasons behind their enormous success.

Another way of thinking about it is that, generally speaking, you don't want to trust your end user to "do the right thing." Yes, you should train them and give them insights, but in the end, they are people. We all forget things that are crucial to our jobs, let alone things that are not. I strongly recommend that security technology evaluations at least include a component of assessing user interaction, aiming for as easy (or as little) as possible. Solutions that promise the moon but depend on users using them correctly are pretty much bound to fail.

Forget the marketing promises.

There is no way around it.

Further, those technologies that prominently prevent end users from doing their jobs (or simply enjoying their work environment) are not only going to fail; they will, without exception, encourage users to find ways to bypass them. The ingenuity of the non-technical employee who wants access to the Dropbox folder with photos of their puppies so that they can show them around is downright astonishing.

Trust me, they will find a way.

In this new world of "IoT," where devices are increasingly connected, where wearables are a reality, a strategy that aims to address security at the end points is delusional at best. You may be able to convince employees to let you manage their personal smartphone, or at least a container inside of the smart device that contains company data; even that is doubtful. What kind of response do you expect to get when you ask them to manage their Internet-connected underwear?

And what would your HR department think of that?

All of this leads us to another very common security management failure. In the preceding chapter, we discussed the notion of "management by compliance," the idea that a company's security efforts must be defined by those security audits that it must successfully pass. The end result is inevitably a slide away from actual security principles and towards auditor bamboozling tactics.

Since we're in the technology chapter, I welcome you to a different, but no less destructive approach: management by vendor.

Look back at that pretty Cisco marketing picture from a few pages back. Its message couldn't be clearer. We know security so well that you should just trust us to deliver it to you. Your house will be in much better order if all your doors are of the same make.

It's a compelling argument, especially in a field where at any given moment, there are thousands of vendors vying for your attention, complete with bombastic claims coupled with highly effective FUD. The RSA conference, one of the most successful technology industry conferences in any field, is no less than a circus, a large stage full of magicians whose tricks prey on our fears. To hear any presentation in RSA is to learn that there is yet another clever way we never thought about in which we can get taken by invisible conmen, or by our own employees, and don't take candy from strangers, ever. It is all so compelling, and security budgets keep growing so fast, that they are soon going to consume half of IT budgets or more (2nd edition note: another prediction that appears to have come true).

We have to protect ourselves!

One of our customer companies, as part of the new security program we helped put in place, asked their legal department to come up with a list of active technology tools vendors in the contract system. We were curious to see the results, because it seemed like there were tools everywhere, often overlapping and even conflicting with each other (just imagine an environment where some security controls innocently weaken other security controls). But even we didn't expect the report to include over 4,000 distinct names.

4,000!

Even if we ignored the human cost, and that the amounts paid were mostly for maintenance and mostly small, the implied waste was enormous.

None of this is sustainable, and it doesn't need to be. But the solution is not to give all the money to the biggest name with the largest portfolio.

Far from it.

In fact, a security-driven argument can be made for heterogeneity in one's infrastructure. It goes like this: the more combinations of technology are in place, the more attack vectors that are necessary to compromise the environment in full. Thus, some resistance is "built in" when there is a mixture of device types, operating systems, and the like. And even big security vendors are prone to failure, as RSA itself demonstrated in 2011, when it became widely known that its highly popular SecureID token authentication system was hacked.

What are we to do, then?

In one sentence, the answer is this: focus on the humans. It is far too easy to get lost in the technical nuances of various security controls, and to get excited by the novelty of another new approach to solving a problem never previously considered. If anything, security marketers are the true experts in their field, doing an amazing job at scratching that itch repeatedly.

But in reality, it is the humans who are fallible, and, more importantly, targeted. It really is quite rare to see a breach suffered entirely via the compromise of technical controls. The weak link in the chain is almost universally related to people and their—our—behaviors and tendencies.

So start there. Put every acquisition through a human filter. Is it something that relies on a hidden assumption about how well people will follow instructions? Does it predicate its success on user cooperation? Then it's probably not a very good technology, no matter how amazing it might sound otherwise.

In technical terms, the goal is to "reduce friction."

Then take a deep breath and let me make another possibly sensational statement: there really is no significant difference between roughly comparable products in any solution class. We can debate all day long about the comparative merits of Checkpoint versus Palo Alto versus Cisco firewalls, but in the end, they all do the same thing pretty well, and what will ultimately make them successful in your organization is not their spec, but rather their *human interface*. In other words, which of these solutions has the most accessible administrator user interface (UI)? Did you remember to ask whether your admins have an established level of comfort with any of them? Because if they do, then that solution should get high marks right there and then. No matter how impressive the technology is, until we get fully autonomous robots/AI to run these things (which is entirely reasonable to expect), it is humans who have to operate them successfully.

Remember that essay about passwords from Chapter 1? By now, is it fair for me to say that I can trust you not to buy into "secure" practices like the one VISA (!) implemented for Visa Checkout? Because here is what they did: they wrote their site such that it is impossible to paste a password into the password field when setting up your account! If you think this is a good security control, you're engaging in the same sort of blind-eye self-delusion of which there is plenty to go around. You see it now, don't you? If you're forcing people to use passwords, then at least encourage them to use a password vault, and allow them to copy and paste their 20-character, random, complex password that includes lookalike characters, is very difficult for a human to type and that was autogenerated by the tool using a good random number generator into the password field. Don't steer them to come up instead with something that is easy for them to type! No matter the theoretical benefit of suppressing the pasting of passwords, it is so overwhelmingly shadowed by the behavioral harm that the result is *less* security, not more.

And now when you read a security standard, I trust that you will start seeing how bad things truly are. Requiring malware protection on every system? Who came up with that genius plan? Some systems simply don't benefit from them, but the number of CentOS virtual machines with a dormant ClamAV package "installed" just to satisfy a compliance checkbox is probably in the millions in AWS alone. It gets downright silly: for serving federal agencies, since some of the best solutions out there aren't approved for use (when I write this, Crowdstrike stands as a good example), using ClamAV becomes a hard requirement. The fact that the package is useless in any normal context other than if the machine is functioning as a file or email server (for the attachments) is apparently lost on the standards authorities, as well as the many enterprise security departments who have this requirement built into their vendor security evaluation matrix. It shows a basic lack of understanding of *both* security *and* people. The former because the package has no possible technical benefit in most contexts. The latter because it assumes that people will not simply install a useless package in order to satisfy a pointless requirement.

Can we please all stop doing that?

And incidentally, we have now come full circle. Yes, technology is an essential component of information security. It is the enabler for the entire field, which would otherwise simply be known as "security". A deep, broad technology background is critical for a CISO to be successful, if only so that they can *resist* the strong temptation to buy everything in sight.

Technology is part of the foundation.

Business experience is another.

And an understanding of human psychology is absolutely crucial.

The 2017 RSA conference was focused on the evolving role of the CISO, including a key presentation about the "role of the CISO in 2020." Do you know what these talks were generally about? The IoT, APIs, and other aspects and impacts of the evolution of technology. Five years and a pandemic later, nothing has changed except for the acronyms.

I ask you, if you've read this far ... how silly is that?

Keep this in mind as we move into our final chapter and redefine the role of the CISO in a way that will, hopefully, make the title of this book moot.

Because failure, as they say, is not an option.

6.2

FOLLYWOOD

As the world of technology becomes ever more abstracted, in some ways it starts to resemble what Hollywood thinks it's supposed to look like. In a way, it's a bit of the sci-fi effect, that is, it's pretty well established that the greatest prophets of our time are sci-fi writers. They have amongst them predicted, with uncanny accuracy, every technological development (and their side effects) in the last few decades, and quite clearly in coming ones as well.

Of course, another way to look at it is simply that their ideas have influenced, and continue to influence, generations of bright, young kids who grow up to become tech entrepreneurs.

On a similar note . . .

Everybody remembers at least one action movie (or MacGyver episode) where the protagonist uses a mirror to reflect a laser in order to bypass a protective grid. They often do it by redirecting the beam to fry some sensor around a corner, taking down the system in the process and gaining unauthorized access to something desirable.

It's such an old Hollywood shtick it's practically a tired one, but we still love it because it's so easy to understand.

Turns out that the very same thing is now happening all over the world of IT. And you should at least know about it, because what it implies is that in the future, we will begin to see cases of a new kind of mistaken identity: one corporation erroneously believing, based on all the evidence at its disposal, that another corporation is attacking it.

This is going to provide all sorts of amusement for, in particular, corporate lawyers. Just imagine this: the CISO goes to the General Counsel (GC) and tells them, factually, that they have incontrovertible proof, with logs and audit trails, that some other company has been

DOI: 10.1201/9781003302759-13

attacking their own systems. As an aside, GCs might want to rewatch *Ghostbusters*, because they will be chasing plenty of apparitions.

Welcome to RAPI attacks. The API part is what it looks like, and the R stands for Reflected; in other words, Reflected API attacks.

And yes, having coined the term, I fully realize how an American audience might read it and recoil in horror. This is one of those moments where I can claim ESL (English as Second Language): it truly never occurred to me. Please pronounce it "ruh-pee" instead of "ray-pee."

Please.

Technobabble aside, this is what it means: in our modern cloud-based world, there are many cloud-based software providers that serve as a sort of enabler or sometimes middleman (we call those middleware) between other organizations. They perform an enormous number of technology functions, and are seemingly growing exponentially in number.

Practically all of them operate with a common set of hidden assumptions. For example, that they are authorized to fulfill their intended function as requested by their users. Sure, it's obvious, but we don't actually spell it out very often. In this case, this hidden assumption has a crucial side-effect: these systems are explicitly authorized to perform their function. Once onboarded, they are *trusted*.

As an aside, there is an entire world in information security and privacy called Zero Trust (ZT) that applies here, and there are some phenomenally bright people (like a fella by the name of Richard Bird) in that world that you can learn from, but for our purposes, that's all I am going to say about ZT. This isn't a technology book, yo.

Back to our narrative: we have cloud systems that are trusted to perform a function with our own corporate systems. Time to discuss the second hidden assumption: we accept that the functionality they provide is, by and large, automated; after all, our purpose in spending money with the vendors is to increase productivity by relying on computers and software to do all sorts of stuff more efficiently than humans can. Just like the first assumption, this is an expectation that isn't explicitly spelled out, but the end result is that these systems are now *trusted* and *automated*.

And now we turn to the third hidden assumption: incentives. By and large, the cloud vendors are typically indemnified against misuse of their own systems and are clearly incentivized to avoid examining what their customers are doing. Liability drives this latter part; by calling themselves a "platform" and leaving the responsibility of proper use of the platform to the customers, the vendors hand off the liability of misuse to the customers. We discussed it earlier, and there is nothing nefarious here. It is the only sane approach for any cloud vendor to take, especially when customers sometimes do horrible and illegal things with free accounts, which happens. A lot. Privacy rules also point in the same direction, as the vendor is directed to not assume ownership of PII that it doesn't need. All of this is usually captured in the commercial paper underlying the engagement.

Which leads us to the finished, three-legged stool: middleware cloud platforms are, by and large, *trusted*, *automated*, and *blind*.

Still with me?

Good.

So now we get to the point, which I am certain you already see.

A malicious actor now has a pretty convenient way to attack any entity indirectly. All they need to do is to "reflect" harmful code through one of these players towards a target, and if they are successful, gain access, while the target thinks that the bad guys (from their perspective) are the legitimate cloud vendor through which the attack was reflected. Just like our protagonist holding a mirror to guide the laser beam to defeat the security system around the corner, so does our hacker.

Let me illustrate this by outlining a benign and trivial, utterly hypothetical, very easy to understand example.

We're all familiar with calendar automation tools—you know, the ones where you connect your corporate calendar to a cloud system that then adds an interface for anyone to book meetings with you at pre-specified time windows. They are very useful and save a tremendous amount of effort for a lot of people.

Here is what they also do: connect directly to corporate groupware (like Google Calendar), with read/write permissions, fully authorized by the user (*trusted*), and often without the knowledge of corporate IT. They always provide a way for the booking party to describe what they wish to discuss ... in a field ... on the booking vendor's web page. Heck, some of them actually allow attachments. The systems don't usually inspect this description, for all the reasons mentioned above; they simply book (*automated*) while handing off the description to the calendaring system of the user (*blind*).

The thing is that *trusting input from users is pretty much the origin of every information security threat.* Every successful hack at some point depends on fooling a system to do something it isn't intended to do in the first place, via malformed input. Even social engineering can be thought of this way, if one thinks of the human operator as the "system" and the con as the fooling (duh).

But what if the corporate calendaring system (not the vendor!) has an unknown exposure in its internal booking engine that can be compromised via a malicious payload in the description field? Then one could "reflect" that payload via the automated external booking vendor and compromise the target system, all the while appearing like it was the vendor that did it. That's certainly what the audit trails will show, if they show anything at all.

Fun, right?

I'll also add that, because APIs are always customized (each one has its own special "language" that it uses), there is no easy way to monitor these interactions—you have to have a behavioral system designed explicitly to learn how each API behaves, and then be able to determine if a malicious payload is being transferred through an authorized connection. Tricky stuff.

This is already happening a fair amount, but the players involved thus far (companies such as Google, AWS, Dropbox and Flickr) appear sophisticated enough to avoid the legal imbroglios. Instead, it's sort of buried in larger and complex conversations about supply-chain kill chains, and zero trust, and this and that, which makes it harder to understand unless you're a total nerd. Seemed like a bit of explanation was in order.

So, anyway ... coffee?

Scenarios like this one are developing at a furious pace, and security vendors are all too happy to remind us of them. Security practitioners are similarly enthused, and why wouldn't they be?

It all adds up to job security.

And since you've stuck around to this point, you can surely see the theme. This stuff is good for the movies, but you can't manage your security program chasing all these shiny objects; RAPI attacks, which were a new idea when I wrote about them, will be considered outdated by the time this edition is available for purchase.

It's great stuff for script-writers, though.

7

THE CISO, REIMAGINED

Still here?

Quite a journey, wasn't it?

We started by disproving the notion that security is a technology discipline, and subsequently ended with a chapter about the critical nature of technology in security. In between, we examined rarely reviewed concepts, like the important role that a good security leader can play in sales and marketing. We discussed two common, and ultimately failing, styles of security management: security by compliance and security by vendor.

What we didn't do yet, however, is provide a future vision. In other words, we now know how security management shouldn't work.

Where does that leave us?

To answer the question, let's attempt to craft a new paradigm.

And there's a second one coming later!

We are building a new structure, and we should start with the foundation. Here is one statement you could insert at the top of your list of criteria for your next CISO three-sixty review, or search, or alternatively, keep in mind when you go for that interview:

> The CISO's role is to enable all parts of the organization to do business successfully without taking on undue technology risk.

That's it. Security is not a guard in front of the gate, although it surely supports the militia.

I like to describe security in the following way: as the CISO, I see my role as *sliding underneath* all the various business units, joining the person who is already there—the legal counsel—in making sure that there are no cracks in the foundations.

 DOI: 10.1201/9781003302759-14

Say what?

Indeed, the CISO is simply the modern incarnation of another highly respected business-wide support function embodied by the legal counsel. The CISO does not replace legal, of course, but they fill a similar role. The legal department addresses legal and liability risk. Security addresses data and technology (liability) risk.

Even better, these two naturally support and rely on each other.

Thought of it this way, one can see a strong connection to the argument about security not being in itself a technology discipline. When operating in a weaker regulatory environment, the role of counsel diminishes, and in a striking parallel, the role of security reduces as well . . . ultimately to a laser focus on technology operations. Just like you don't need a highly paid chief counsel when bribery of government officials allows you to succeed regardless of your actual business practices, so do you not need a CISO when all your technology risk lies in the proper implementation of firewalls.

In these cases, what you really need are a consigliere and a good hacker, respectively.

But for those of us making a living in less corrupt environments, I think it's fair to say that risk is generally tied to business operations, and that in the modern world, the latter is highly reliant on technology use. Since you're still reading, I hope that by now I have illustrated to you that

- If you're a CISO, you're (probably) going about it wrong.
- If you manage a CISO, you're (probably) going about it wrong.
- If you're hiring a CISO, you're (probably) going about it wrong.

Let me inject another simple statement here:

A CISO—no matter how talented—without a solid business operations background is unable to evaluate threats to the business.

Point blank period.

If you don't understand how cash flows through the pipeline of a modern business, how customers are acquired and lost, how debt is managed, and all the other little things that make this thing called a "company" run, then you are by definition incapable of understanding and evaluating risk to the operations of said company.

It's nothing against you.

You're simply out of your depth.

Security is about managing risk—I'm not revealing anything here that you didn't know before. There is simply no way anyone can manage risk when they do not have a finely tuned understanding of the sources of risk *in their proper business context*.

Business context.

NOT technology context.

One fascinating cumulative side effect of this search for the "brilliant technologist" security leader; their inevitable failure due to the overwhelming odds stacked against them; their wrong positioning within the organizational hierarchy (often reporting to the CTO or CIO); and the lack of organizational insight into how a CISO can play a positive business role within the organization is this: in so many organizations, it is now the default (even if unstated) expectation that CISOs will not last too long, even *while they are being hired*.

How incredibly cynical is that? And how sad?

Worse, those that occupy the position instinctively grasp this expectation and prepare themselves for it, for if they are anything, stupid they are not. It is a destructive cycle, and the results are predictable. Is it any wonder that security departments often engage in so much CYA, that it becomes their primary mode of communications with everybody else?

Consider.

On one hand, you have increasing pressure from regulators and the markets, translated *regularly and incorrectly* through company boards as a "mandate to protect the company against hackers," leading to a war mentality of sorts. All of that is occurring in an endlessly evolving (if I am allowed to continue the analogy here) theater of operations.

On the other hand, you have highly trained and skilled professionals in their field, who are placed in a position where they need to navigate (to them) foreign waters while developing, implementing, and executing a plan whose success is ultimately outside of their control. Security, at least in the context of hacking, is an uneven war, where the attacker can try forever and needs to succeed only once, whereas the defender must never be wrong. But even putting that aside, the internal forces that rely on these individuals performing their duties have even more urgent needs to satisfy, such as dealing with ever-increasing competitive pressure and the constant possibility of rapid shifts in their markets.

I mean, just look at what is still happening in retail.

And let's not talk about what happened to taxis because of ride-sharing.

Is it any wonder that an average CISO doesn't last too long in their position? That the industry is a revolving door? And with this in mind, does it in fact surprise you that often, hiding behind the pretty words, there is a sort of mutual understanding on both sides of the equation (if you will) that the *CISO is the designated fall guy* if ever something goes wrong?

I call this phenomenon the *discardable CISO*. In essence, it is the perfect encapsulation of this failed trajectory: we hire somebody to give us the cover we need, the proof that we take all this stuff seriously, until the inevitable happens—and then we can fire them for failing in their job.

It really is just lack of experience that leads to so few CISOs insisting on hefty contractual termination payments or golden parachutes, although I am seeing them pop up more regularly these days. A 2nd edition note here: this has not yet panned out *quite* as much as I thought it would, mostly because CISOs simply don't have enough leverage to demand these in contract. More on that in a bit.

Speak to professionals in the field, those who are experienced CISOs or are on the CISO track. You will soon find out that this role can plausibly be considered the most depressing of all for executives. They never get the recognition they deserve, except when things go wrong, at which point they must revert to the philosophical approach that all publicity is good publicity, or quit.

All this brings up another hugely important issue, which is that there is no obvious career path progression for the CISO.

After all, even assuming they somehow make it through a few years (as the good ones will admit, through sheer blind luck), where would the CISO go? What is their next step? They can't replace their natural boss, be it the CFO or general counsel, because they are unqualified and untrained for those jobs. If they happen to report to the CIO, then they could conceivably step up to that role, but it will be difficult to manage politically, especially after years of being the person "in charge of saying no." Indeed, a typical CISO without good exposure to business roles such as sales, marketing, and finance really has nowhere to go in the organization. At least not readily.

If that isn't a testament to just how frivolously companies take this role, regardless of the "C" in CISO, I don't know what is.

Let me ask you something else: how often does your head of sales interview prospective CISOs? And if you asked them to, and even if they acquiesced, would they even know what to ask? I bet they would look at you funny.

Maybe I'm going too far. How about your chief counsel? Head of HR?

As you have read this book, I believe you may have gotten an idea of how to avoid this fate. The solution can be summarized in the classic three-bullet-point format:

- *Don't Just Hire Technical.* Do not focus overly much on the technical background of your CISO. Instead, focus on their capabilities to become well-rounded executives, with a good understanding of human and business operational risk. Yes, a good CISO has to have a superior technology background. But if you can find one that also has actual experience managing profit and loss (P&L), that should perk your ears for the upcoming interview. And remember, the goal is that compliance will take care of itself, so while they will need to possess demonstrable expertise in the particular regulations impacting your organization, it simply cannot be the focus of their job. Here is a little test you can use to see if your CISO has the right mindset—find out if they can envision writing a narrative risk assessment that includes (gasp!) no tables or charts whatsoever. The point here is that a technical risk assessment, which is unfortunately what the vast majority of the industry believes is the desired end result, pretty much requires the use of at least some tables, because it focuses on attack vectors and has to organize them somehow in order to evaluate them to any reasonable degree. If you ever looked at one . . . well, let's just say many people hate these kinds of assessments for a reason. An assessment focused instead on the business risks *resulting from the use of technology* doesn't require any of that, and also naturally lends itself towards a narrative format. Even better, they can be kept short,* and should be easy to digest by, say (another gasp!), a board member. If your CISO cannot successfully articulate risk in simple *business* terms, then they don't really deserve that "C." And if their analysis highlights human factors, then you have yourself a winner.

- *Reenvision the CISO Role.* Instead of hiring a discardable CISO, consider your new executive hire as an important member of the business leadership team. Their role will be a supporting one, certainly, just like counsel's. Specifically, they would need to be able to highlight the risks involved in significant business decisions that arise from the use of technology. As we covered in the legal chapter, this can extend to every area, including technology acquisition and implementation, cloud use, potential regulatory challenges, and, yes, mergers and acquisitions (M&A). A CISO thus placed can be perfectly positioned to provide a sanity check to the organization—not to stop business from happening, but to avoid making a critical error that could become extremely costly down the road. The "Department of How" instead of the "Department of No." But they need the right background to be able to function at this level! (see point 1). As a side benefit, a CISO who is successful in this revised role is also a natural candidate for the board, at least as an advisor.
- *Hire with Intent.* Even security people get bored of security, eventually. If you are hiring a brilliant person to fill this important role, try to think about where they may be able to advance. And then make sure that they get a line of reporting to the person currently holding that position.

Who should it be? My opinion is that *the COO makes a natural, logical next step*. They both have an internal organizational focus, are operational and risk driven, and must work to be in harmony with

---

* My own approach is to figure out the appropriate, broad risk categories for the organization—typically 6–8—and then cover each one in a single page. My feeling is that if you cannot communicate risk in that much space, then you are too far down in the weeds already.

all parts of the organization, since their duty is to make it operate as smoothly as possible. Security leaders, like COOs, have a natural tendency to "listen to the heartbeat" of operations, the optimization of the management of routine tasks, and the detection of when those exhibit or develop unexpected weaknesses.

And yes, clearly I am proposing that the CISO's natural progression path is similar to that of the CIO. There is nothing wrong with that, and it places the CISO in their proper position as a peer of the CIO. By serving as a shadow risk manager, occasional paralegal, board advisor, and part-time brand manager, the CISO of the future must be considered in the running for this ultimate internally facing role, the chief operating officer.

Plus a bit of added internal competition never hurts. I betcha that Jack Welch said that once or twice.

Note that the unique perspective of the CISO brings something special to the table. We discussed the value of negative inference thinking. Another critical component that is common to every good CISO is strong rapid decision-making capabilities. They must have an ability to function well and keep a cool head under fire, for one. If you are in the midst of dealing with a security incident, or worse, a confirmed breach, the sign of an excellent CISO is their *apparent lack of panic*. While everyone else is tearing their hair out, fear is running rampant, and the tendency is to shut everything down, it is the job of the CISO to assess the situation calmly and propose a course of action that will not only "fix it now," but direct tasks like preserving the chain of evidence (for possible prosecution later), containing the problem without alerting the intruder too early so as to increase the chances of their identification, determining the point of engagement with law enforcement (and regulators), working with strategic customers, and interacting with the media. They must have the relationships, credibility, and trust necessary to execute under tremendous stress, and the expertise and knowledge to guide and utilize limited resources in the most effective way to solve big issues, all the while avoiding costly and irreparable mistakes.

All pretty good qualities to have in a future number two.

None of this will happen, of course, if our candidate pool continues to studiously avoid business training, and instead focus on getting their way with fear, uncertainty, and doubt.

To take this even further, let me suggest that a good security leader should be highly personable, if not downright jovial. I like to joke, but with more than just a hint of truth, that when acting in the role, I get to be the silliest guy in the room.

Why?

Because by virtue of the position, everybody is afraid of the CISO. The default expectation is that the security head will be severe, intimidating, and frustrating to work with.

Have you watched any Hollywood movies depicting these folks?

We did it to ourselves.

So, my dear CISO colleagues, I urge you to break the mold. Be funny. Crack a joke at your own expense, especially when the tension is high. Nobody will expect it, and it will allow everyone to let out that secret sigh of relief. You'd be shocked at how much easier your job will become.

Alright. Let's summarize all of this, shall we?

Take a deep breath. Here we go.

A good CISO will

- Understand their role is an ultimate support function for *every part* of the organization.
- Grasp the nature of such support as related to management of business risk arising from the use of technology, as opposed to technology risk arising from operational decisions.
- Be *ready* and *eager* to engage with non-technical business units.
- Have a business operations background, or express a strong desire to develop one.
- Everyone, please, please send your CISO to business school. That MBA will do both of you a load of good. At the very least have them *take a psychology class*. Not to sound dramatic, but that may well be the most important career skill they will ever attain.
- Exhibit the tendencies that would make them a prospect for the role of COO, and, ideally, be highly personable.

Last but not least, reset those expectations!

Stop treating this role as something "you have to deal with." Take advantage of the contrarian thinking that security pros come with, built-in. It's a feature, not a bug. Give them the context they need to expand their thinking from the world of "IT security" (I hereby admit that this is one term I truly despise) and into the world of business security.

And collectively, let's all take a deep breath and relax. The world is moving fast, true. But the wheels are not coming off the wagon, and the principles remain the same. Security is simply an emerging discipline, that's all.

It serves a crucial purpose, surely.

But it isn't unique.

I hope this book helps you shortcut through the next few years of frustration dealing with everything security—as a practitioner, a colleague, or a supervisor, or even from a casual point of interest.

And at the very least . . . I hope you were entertained.

Wait! There's more.

Keep reading!

7.2

A New Paradigm

While the original book, even to my own surprise, appears even more valid today than it was when I first wrote it, my own understanding of the underlying principles has continued to evolve.

Especially two key ones.

One of them suggests another new paradigm, but I'll keep that for last.

First, and perhaps the toughest to tackle, is about the future of the CISO. As in, is there a future for this role?

Let me get the big statement out of the way:

No.

There isn't.

The current incarnation of the standalone CISO role as part of the executive committee is, in a business sense, simply unnecessary. And as soon as senior corporate leaders grow comfortable enough—as in less fearful—to realize security is not the grave danger to their world that they are currently being bullied into thinking, they will do something about it. Then the job will diminish, and in many places, simply disappear.

Phew.

Now that I put that in print . . . let me see if I can convince you it has merit.

Clearly if you have read this book to this point, you already know that I take a dim view of the CISO as some sort of distinct technology savant. While this is indeed the way many CISOs conduct themselves, it doesn't mean that it's the desired outcome, only that they currently wield a fairly heavy bully stick.

For one thing, companies already have two senior technology leaders in their ranks: the CTO and the CIO. There is another rising

DOI: 10.1201/9781003302759-15

star here on the engineering side, which is the CPO—Chief Product Officer—and a new joint title that has emerged to help the CEO keep their reports down a reasonable number: the CPTO, or Chief Product and Technology Officer.

Remember the discussion earlier about how a business-oriented CISO (the best kind!) might position themselves as COO candidates?

While I believe that it is a good way for smart CISOs to align themselves towards greater things in their career, I have a more natural proposition for how such a progression might occur. To tear away at the fourth wall for a moment, I've been kicking myself for a few years for not having written it explicitly when this book first came out.

It seemed even wilder than the rest of the crazy stuff I wrote.

The solution is actually really super simple, even if it comes across as counter-intuitive.

Here we go.

Good CIOs manage technology *and risk* already. They seem to have disappeared from the scene in recent years, except in large enterprises. Who hires CIOs anymore when everything is in the cloud? You might get yourself a head of IT—a CIO in anything but title, and a downgraded salary—to manage all these cloud vendors.

This dynamic also ties perfectly with the explosive rise of the CISO, who in many organizations who have them are, as we have illustrated, nowhere near having the kind of business and operational experience to really be an executive. But they fill a need, albeit a temporary one.

What, you think it isn't temporary?

Alright. Go back in time to the late Nineties or early Naughties and ask people whether CIOs will be important in the future. Go ahead, I dare you.

In fact, the important point here is that many of the modern crop of CISOs would have likely become CIOs thirty years ago.

So let's tie this all together, and reimagine these roles in the only sensible, lasting way.

The standalone CIO title is kinda headed out the door.

The standalone CISO title is similarly going to deflate to its natural size.

But technology is ever more important to every company.

So what are we to do? There has to be a way to square the circle.

The solution is already evident.

Take a careful look around, and you will see that these roles are naturally merging. Plenty of companies now hire a "Head of Security and IT." It's an actual trend in Silicon Valley, for one thing.

So can we rip the band-aid and let them merge?

They will have a new but very familiar title:

The CISO.

Wait, what?

Well, I actually mean it to look like this instead: CI/SO.

Not Chief Information Security Officer.

Rather, the Chief Information AND Security Officer (just like the CPTO).

And everything will make sense again.

The second key principle, and the driver of a new paradigm, is an insight gained after decades of helping so many executives in so many companies grapple with the gap between expectations and reality around security.

Let's unpack that a little.

The dynamics are always very human. Many senior corporate leaders don't want to do much about security unless they're forced to, which is the chief complaint of security people. The minority, who had the pleasure of dealing with an uncomfortable security incident, often swing towards doing way too much, because they don't have a choice in those moments. Then they pretend to care for a while, until the external noise dies down or they grow tired of the whole circus (or simply leave).

This feast or famine culture in security is endemic, and as we have illustrated in different contexts, a prescription for failure. Or at least job dissatisfaction, operational fatigue and depression.

But there is a way to reimagine the scary parts of security in a simple way, that is easily understandable to all other senior corporate leaders, makes sense in a business context, and naturally helps calibrate and right-size security efforts.

I mean it.

Extremely simple.

It comes from the world of retail, and it's called *shrinkage*.

Shrinkage, in case you don't know, is the catchall euphemism used in retail to describe mismatches between store inventory and book (recorded) inventory due to shoplifting, employee theft, fraud, admin errors, and the like.

There is a direct one-to-one match between shrinkage categories and security fears. For example, hackers can be thought of as shoplifters. Internal threats? Employee theft. Admin errors and fraud? Well . . . admin errors and fraud.

But here's the thing: people in retail understand that shrinkage is part of life. You're gonna face some losses, and you can never entirely prevent them; your goal is to *reasonably minimize* them. Shrinkage is expressed in a percentage of the bottom line (that number was 1.62% in 2020).

And what does *reasonably minimize* mean?

Because the point is that, once you come to accept that some losses are inevitable (because there are always going to be shoplifters, misbehaving employees, fraudulent activities and vendors, etc.), then you would be willing to spend only enough money to reduce shrinkage by at least that much. You certainly wouldn't want to spend $120 to reduce your shrinkage by $100; that would be dumb.

Hold on, Barak. What does this have to do with security?

Pretty much everything.

Because right now we're doing things in security like spending $2000 to reduce $100 worth of exposure. Why are we doing it? Because we don't have a good handle on what the exposure really is like, and there are a bunch of people whose job is to make us feel like that $100 worth of exposure is actually $5000 worth of exposure.

And they are really good at their job

Yes, yes, I've heard it all: "it is impossible to measure ROI in security" is the most common objection. It's only impossible because we don't want to do it, and that's usually because the people who are supposed to do it can't be bothered to learn how to do it, and they don't have to: they can simply scare you into paying.

You know who they are.

The vendors aren't helping, either, because of self-interest; their goal is to sell you their product, so their ROI calculators are (correctly) not received at face value.

In reality, the data (like the cost of breaches) has been accruing and is far more available now than it used to be.

But let me tell you something: without going into an in-depth analysis of every expense, once you have business operations experiences, it isn't that hard to tie expense line items into business goals, or possible losses, and even come up with rough numbers around them. Every other executive has to do that.

The key point here, though, is a different one.

Ready?

It's that we need to accept that some losses are inevitable.

Take a deep breath, and read that again.

We need to accept that some security-related losses are inevitable.

Just keep them reasonable.

Yes, I realize I am not truly saying anything shocking; in theory, all these fancy security standards purport to say the same thing when they go into the realm of (in particular, quantitative) risk assessment. I call shenanigans; nobody treats them that way on the ground. They just try to come up with some high/medium/low rankings and then fix the highs, cost be damned. Funny how the *Hooman Operating System* is so remarkably consistent.

It's the whole point behind cyber-resilience—the idea that, by accepting that we will go down at some point, we focus efforts on having good, speedy ways to safely recover, in order to minimize the damage. Once you get into this mindset, you stop being afraid of breaches and incidents and the monsters under the bed, and go about your business secure in the knowledge that no matter what, you'll be alright.

In fact, the only real problem with *cyber-resilience* is that the term itself is a bit of a tongue-twister, so it turns people off.

Security Shrinkage is so much easier.

And no, it's not a *Seinfeld* reference, but if you can't get over that famous George Constanza scene, then perhaps *Digital Shrinkage* would work for you.

Just agree—really agree—that there is some acceptable loss to the business related to all this security stuff, measure it, and try to align expectations with reality. It's a much more sensible approach than "preventing all the bad thingz from happening."

You can't do that, anyway.

This pragmatic approach to security is the thread that runs through this entire text.

It puts security in perspective.

And let me tell you . . .

Perspective in security is something we all seem to have lost.

Let's get it back, shall we?

Printed in the United States
by Baker & Taylor Publisher Services